Camino de Santiago Guide to Preparing Well
&
Saving Money 2.0

By
Helen Van Wagenen

*"Trustworthy Advice for
the Journey Ahead"*

Dedication

We are thankful for the millions who have gone before us

on the Camino, sowing thoughts and prayers

for nearly two millennia, and we dedicate this book

to those who will someday walk.

May you find who you are meant to be,

and what you are meant to do for the rest of your journey.

For God's Glory.

Buen Camino.

Acknowledgements

We are grateful to the *peregrinos* (pilgrims) who have given us advice through the years, and for the strenuous, majestic, comical, and glorious experiences we have shared, which perhaps will be written down in other books. This "2.0 edition" of our guidebook is the distillation of our knowledge, your feedback, and new information. Our goal is to help more and more people walk the Camino de Santiago, or at least think and live like pilgrims.

Helen Van Wagenen

It All Started for Us in 2007...

We founded Camino Provisions and wrote this book to help you prepare well and save money as you make your plans to walk the *Camino de Santiago* (Way of St. James). In the early spring of 2007 we first heard about the Camino. We learned what we could on the internet and from guidebooks, sifting through information in several languages to find out what we could, which wasn't much. In the years since then, two generations of our family have walked many Camino journeys in different seasons of the year, and we have pilgrim-minded friends all over the world.

In this *Guide* is the essence of what our Camino Provisions team have distilled from everything we have read, heard, and experienced about the Camino. Simply put, we present favorite money-and-time-saving information to help you plan and prepare for *your* trip. We sift through and review resources and products for you. We post regular articles on our website and social media with tips, gear reviews, and news updates about the Camino, because we know most of you do not have the time or know the resources to trust to get answers.

All visitors to our website can access loads of resources, including our *Gear Reviews* page with our favorite Camino-tested items. Trust us when we say that if we recommend an item, it is in our Camino backpack! Follow the links to shop for your Camino needs. We are Amazon affiliates, which means when you follow our links to the Amazon product page, and other online stores, they give us a small commission if you buy something. We turn around and give back through **Provisions With Purpose,** by donating to non-profit groups helping Camino pilgrims.

Now let's get *YOU* started on your plans for the most life-giving walk ever!

Buen Camino,

Helen

Table of Contents

Make Your Plans

Movies and stories you hear or read from returning *peregri-nos* (pilgrims) may have given you the inaccurate impression that there is only one route, and one way to walk the Camino de Santiago. We are going to tell you our favorite ways to personalize your plans to fit your schedule, season, budget, and fitness level. Which route do I walk? When do I travel? How do I plan the trip? These are the same questions we had when we began our search years ago, and it was very difficult to find the answers. We wrote this book and founded Camino Provisions to guide you to realistic goals and practical approaches to walking the Camino de Santiago.

Which Route?

While the most well known route, the *Camino Francés*, covers 500 miles from St. Jean Pied-de-Port, France to Santiago de Compostela, Spain, there are many other official pilgrimage routes. All of them wind through beautiful country, all with wonder and adventure around every corner, all ending in the beautiful ancient city of Santiago de Compostela.

Some are shorter and some are longer distances. If you have unlimited time, consider starting from farther away or spending extra days to explore some of the amazing cities along the route. If your time is short, choose a shorter route, or a section of a route. If you want to earn a *compostela,* a certificate issued by the Catholic Church to those walking for religious reasons, you will need to walk at least the final 100km of any of the official routes, and present your official *peregrino credenciál* that has been stamped and dated at each stop along your walk to Santiago. Other routes are being approved all along, but here are some favorite routes with their approximate distances:

Beginning in France

Camino* Francés: St. Jean to Santiago, 790k (500mi)

Chemin* de Paris: Paris to St. Jean, 1000k (621mi)

Chemin de Vézelay: Vézelay to St. Jean, 900k (559mi)

Chemin de Le Puy: Le Puy to St. Jean, 740k(459mi)

Chemin de Arles: Arles to Somport Pass, 750k (466mi)

Beginning in Spain & Portugal

Via de la Plata: Seville to Santiago, 1,000k (621mi)

Camino del Norte: Irun to Santiago, 830k (515mi)

Camino Primitivo: Oviedo to Melide, 320k (198mi)

Camino Portugués: Oporto to Santiago, 240k (149mi)

Camino Portugués: Lisbon to Oporto, 370k (229mi)

Camino Inglés: Ferrol to Santiago, 110k (68mi)

Favorite departure cities on the Camino Francés with distances that earn a compostela (100k)

Pamplona to Santiago, 710k (441mi)

Burgos to Santiago, 500k (311mi)

León to Santiago, 315k (195mi)

Sarría to Santiago, 115k (71mi)

Favorite add-on routes

Santiago to Finisterre, 90k (56mi)

Santiago to Muxía, 70k (43mi)

Santiago to Finisterre to Muxía to Santiago, 188k (117mi)

*Camino is the Spanish for "way", and *chemin* is French for "path."

How to Get to Favorite Departure Points

Getting to the city that will be the starting point of your Camino journey can be pretty confusing if you are new to travel in Europe. The Rome2rio.com website or app is free, and is a great resource to find out how to get from any "Point A" to any "Point B." It lets you plug in a departure city and destination city and gives you all the options for traveling from one to the other—buses, trains, airplanes, and cars— and provides links and estimated costs for each option. Here are our recommendations to get to favorite departure points on the Camino Frances. A tip for you about taking the bus is that non-Europeans might find it impossible to make reservations online, so plan on getting your tickets at the bus company ticket window as soon as you arrive at the station, as some buses fill up quickly.

To St. Jean Pied-de-Port FR—

+ Fly to Paris and take the TGV(France's bullet train,https://www.sncf.com/en/passenger-offer/travel-by-train/tgv/tgv-offer) to Bayonne; allow for time to get from the CDG airport to the TGV train station, and choose service that does not have frequent stops for the fastest, most efficient travel; Transfer to the local train (https://www.sncf.com/en) that goes from Bayonne to SJPP; plan an "open jaw" ticket, traveling from the North America to Paris and then returning to North America from Santiago de Compostela through Madrid. Or...

+ Fly to London and take the Stansted Express Train to the London-Stansted airport to take a Ryanair flight to Biarritz, FR; take a bus or taxi to SJPP. Fly home from Santiago through Madrid on an "open jaw" ticket. Or fly Santiago to London-Stansted on Ryanair and back home from London.

+ It is also possible to travel from Pamplona to SJPP or Roncesvalles, so if you get a good deal on a flight to Madrid, you can stop over then fly, train or bus to Pamplona, and go by taxi from there.

To Pamplona, Spain—

+ Fly to Madrid, and then fly to Pamplona.

+ Fly to Madrid, take a Renfe train ((www.renfe.com/EN/viajeros/) to Pamplona.

+ Fly to Madrid, take an Alsa bus from T4 ((www.alsa.es/en) or PLM Autocares bus (www.plmautocares.com) to Pamplona.

To Sarría, Spain—

+ Fly to Madrid, then take the Alsa bus from T4 (www.alsa.es/en/our-destinations) to Lugo, then the Monbus (www.monbus.es/en) to Sarría. There is some Alsa bus service from the Madrid airport.

+ Fly to Madrid, Renfe train (www.renfe.com/EN/viajeros/) or Alsa bus to León, bus to Sarría.

When to Go?

Everyone has favorite seasons, types of weather, and temperatures. You either enjoy being around lots of people, or fewer people. Travel costs, crowds, and availability of accommodations vary with the seasons. Here is what you need to know about each season on the Camino to help you decide what will suit you best.

The weather across northern Spain is VERY diverse. In recent years on the *Camino Francés* we have encountered everything from sleet and temperatures in the 20'sF crossing the Pyrenees in mid May, to scorching heat in the 90'sF in summer between Burgos and León on the *Meseta*, to rain so heavy that *peregrinos* needed to stop every hour to take off their boots and empty out the water. To find out the range of temperatures and rainfall throughout the year use your Internet browser to search, "annual weather in Burgos, Spain" (or whatever city you want to research along the route you are considering) and several helpful weather websites will pop up with lots of information.

As you might expect, weather is one of the main factors affecting the Camino experience. Therefore it is also one of the determining factors for the number of *peregrinos* walking at any given time. If you want a more peaceful walk in spring, with fewer *peregrinos* on the Camino and fewer tourists in the cities, March, April and early May might suit you best. Airfares and other travel should be cheaper in this "shoulder season" (not "peak season" and not "off season"), and seasonally driven accommodations and cafés generally open the week after Easter to begin receiving guests. Daytime temperatures are nice for walking, nights can be cool, and you will undoubtedly encounter a number of rainy days. Spring flowers, crops and trees are bursting everywhere. Autumn provides a similar peace and absence of crowds. Albergues and hostels are generally open through October. Airfares drop in price after the demands of peak summer travel, and it's harvest time on the farms and vineyards along the Camino. September and much of October have less rain than the spring. In general, pilgrims walking in spring and autumn are people who are not restricted by a school or university calendar.

If you like hot weather, lots of people, and excitement, then summer will suit you best. The temperatures will be the warmest of the year in July and August, and the demographics of the Camino shift to include an increase of high school and college age students on their summer breaks. Accommodations may be *completo* (no vacancy) and even food and water supplies can be strained to accommodate the swell in numbers. May and June are also becoming busier because of the increased numbers during the rest of the summer. Travel costs are higher in the summer because of the higher demand for flights, train, and bus services. If you are limited to travel during the summer, but are hoping for fewer people, consider walking one of the less travelled routes. The *Camino Norte, Camino Portugués,* and *Camino Inglés* are becoming new favorites with summertime pilgrims who hope for more quiet.

If you like cold weather and solitude you might prefer a winter trip. Travel costs will be the cheapest of the year, but you will need more gear, and many albergues and other pilgrim-driven services are closed. Plan for less daylight, which means fewer hours of sunlit walking.

Spanish Holidays

The people of Spain celebrate their holidays well. They enjoy clos-
ing up their businesses to be with family and friends. We have
been the *peregrinos* standing outside a shop asking, "Why in the
world is this store closed today?" And the ones finding out the reason all the beds are full in Santiago is because of a national holiday.
Not only are many places closed on the calendar holiday itself, but
in some cities an extra day might be added to the holiday obser-
vance if the holiday lands on a Tuesday or Thursday. Mondays and
Fridays are then known as "bridge days," and often are not listed
on Spanish national calendars. In general, cafés, restaurants, and
lodging will be open on holidays, because they serve tourists traveling to other cities to enjoy the celebrations. However, grocery
stores, *mercados*, bakeries, and other businesses catering to the
local residents **do close** on holidays. The following list is not total-
ly inclusive, since some cities add celebrations for their individual
patron saints and such, but these are the most widely celebrated
holidays across Spain to help you plan your trip.

- New Year's Day

- January 6, Epiphany (known as *Dia de los Reyes,* Kings Day)

- Easter (and other days of Holy Week, *Semana Santa,* like Maun-
  dy Thursday and Good Friday, prior to Easter Sunday)

- May 1, Labor Day

- Late May-Early June, Ascension Day (Santiago celebrates this
  holiday for a week or more, but stores are usually only closed
  on the Day itself)

- June 25 St. James Day in Santiago

- July 6-14 (*Sanfermines,* "running of the Bulls" in Pamplona)

- October 12, National Holiday

- November 1, All Saints Day

- December 6, Constitution Day

- December 8, Immaculate Conception Day

- Christmas Day

Your Lodging Plan

You might have the impression that the only places to stay as you walk the Camino are the big dormitory style albergues in the movie *The Way*. There is actually a range, including public and private, cheap and pricey. Here is our guidance so you can decide what to expect and what type will suit you best. At the cheapest end of the spectrum are camping and the municipal albergues, and at the expensive end of the spectrum are hotels or apartment rentals. Our team's collective experiences include all types of sleeping arrangements. In the spirit of doing what is right for you, choose what will fit your budget and allow you to get the sleep you need each night. Not every type of lodging is available at every stop, so a willingness to be flexible will serve you well, and will help you make some good memories.

Campgrounds are not available everywhere, and you must get permission and sometimes pay a fee to camp on private property along the Camino. You also have to carry all the equipment you will need if you camp, adding weight to your pack.

Municipal albergues are run by the government and usually are a large dormitory style room with as many bunk beds lined up as will fit the space. Bathrooms are often communal with both genders sharing common space, and hopefully, but not always, with curtains or doors on shower and toilet stalls. You may be guided to a bed that is literally right beside someone you do not know. For some of us this might be a way to make a new friend, but for others this might be a nightmare. The cost varies from 3-8€ per night, not including any food. Some places have the facility and staff to offer an evening meal and continental breakfast for additional cost.

Amenities at private albergues vary, but usually include fewer people sharing space, and nicer facilities in general. They charge 10-15€ for the night. Sometimes you can stay in a small room with just two or three bunk beds, with a shared private bathroom serving 10-12 people. A few newer albergues have a couple of private rooms available at a bit more cost.

Pensions, and small hotels offer the most economical private rooms. Some will have private bathrooms en suite. The price range is 20-35€.

The most expensive accommodations on the Camino include five star hotels like the famous Spanish luxury chain Parador, and apartment rentals reserved through online service companies like AirBnB.com. Rooms and amenities carry price tags matching their splendor, but even the Paradors have a frequent user program with which you can earn free nights. Details in **"Where to Stay."**

Camino Tour Companies

Companies are available that provide travel services for *peregrinos* in setting up accommodations for your journey based on an agreed upon itinerary. Solo and group experiences are available. While none of our team have used one of these services—yes, they do charge a fee—we have met many pilgrims who were using one of these companies, and most of them seemed pleased with their decisions. Having a set itinerary like this does take some of the spontaneity out of your experience, but many people would never even attempt to walk the Camino without this type of help and assurance. Our opinion: whatever it takes to get you on your way, DO IT!

How Long Will It Take Me?

In order to answer this question and guide you, we have to ask you to do some self-evaluation about your health, fitness level, and reasons for walking the Camino. Finishing well, injury free, and in the time you have set aside for your journey, is what we propose as a general goal for everyone. It is difficult for most people to duplicate the daily physical demands of a pilgrimage while at home, because most people can't spend the time walking 5-6 hours per day. It is difficult to assess what you will be able to sustain day after day on the Camino. Recovery time will be different for everyone after a day's hard walk, and getting enough sleep to walk a full day every day is a challenge for many people.

To help you figure out your sustainable walking pace we have devised an exercise for you to complete. Try this to find your pace after your doctor has cleared you to do this kind of exercise. Some day soon, chart a three-mile walking route over varied terrain near your home. Allow several hours in your schedule to complete this exercise. Wear regular trainer shoes or comfortable walking shoes if you don't have your hiking footwear yet. Walk at a comfortable pace, taking as many breaks as you need to finish. Time yourself from start to finish. Carry a liter of water and 10 pounds of weight in a pack (if you don't have one, borrow something; it doesn't have to be a particularly good fit for this exercise; use a couple of 5 pound bags of flour or something to simulate the weight of your gear). If your time allows it walk the same route again, timing yourself. And again. And again. See if you can complete 3 to 5 circuits of this three-mile course. Walk at a comfortable pace, and stop before or when you have pain any where in your body. Note how you feel afterwards and the following day. Do you feel sore anywhere? What was your pace? (Divide the number of minutes it took you to walk three miles by three.) At that pace, how many miles could you walk in four hours? We have found that averaging between 2-3 mph is a sustainable walking speed for 5-6 hours per day. Fatigue, food, and call of nature breaks will add to your time. Adjust your number of days or the number of miles to accommodate your pace and calendar. Please do NOT try to quicken your pace or push yourself into an injured state in which you have to quit walking early. Our recommendations are in **"Your Footwear System."**

Favorite Guidebooks

If you are reading this Guidebook, you are getting some of the best, most recently published information available in English about walking the Camino. We continue to road test products, talk to pilgrims, and walk the Camino ourselves in order to provide the best advice on every Camino topic. We have our ears to the ground to keep tabs on what is happening that affects pilgrims. We post anything new we learn between editions of the Guidebook on FaceBook @CaminoProvisions and our website.

For the nitty-gritty route information, including elevation charts and mileage, John Brierley's, ***A Pilgrim's Guide to the Camino de Santiago*** is still our favorite, and only available in print form. It is updated every year, so make sure you note the date of printing for the copy you consider buying or borrowing. The author updates changes in route, and also gives some updated information about accommodations. In order to keep your pack weight lower, if you choose Brierley's book or another one that is only in print form, we recommend scanning or photographing pages of the book that you want to reference, and keeping these image files on your smart phone. Not in the cloud, but accessible without wifi. If you bring the print copy, use scissors to cut unnecessary pages from your copy which will reduce the weight significantly. Do NOT tear out the pages, because this may loosen all the remaining pages from the spine and render your book harder to use. You may want to consider Brierley's new Kindle book, ***Camino de Santiago Maps: St. Jean Pied de Port - Santiago de Compostela***. This digital guide includes all of Brierley's good maps, elevations and route information, as well as a list of albergues with phone numbers and costs, and important historic monuments and buildings in each town. You will need the free Kindle app on your smart phone which will allow you to access a Kindle formatted book. Note: With this or any other guidebook, you need to travel at your best pace, which may not be the daily distances suggested by the author. In fact, our favorite guide to first aid on the Camino says, "the biggest cause of injury on the Camino is guidebooks!" (Tom & Em Hill, *Camino First Aid*, free download from our website).

We recommend our *Guide* for excellent advice about the Camino. John Brierley's guide is good for maps and route info, but the Camino is so well marked now, you may not need it. Many people use his book, so a good strategy about planning where to stop for the night is to stop before or after Brierley's suggested stopping places, since those trying to follow his suggestions may be filling up all the beds.

Many good Camino forums are online where people submit questions and receive a variety of answers, but beware of being overwhelmed with too many opinions and misinformation. One of the reasons we began Camino Provisions was because of our personal experiences searching and not finding accurate information when planning our first walk. For the novice, it is difficult to discern what advice to follow from comments on forums, and you may not know enough to know what to ask. Our advice is put together by our family and trusted friends of varying ages and fitness levels. We will tell you *why* we advise what we do, and give you enough information for you to decide what is right for you.

What to Budget Including Free Airfare Summary

Follow our tips for free airfares and discounts and you might not have to put off walking the Camino for as long as you might think! These are not shady gimmicks, or fake fares, they are legitimate and real, and our readers have saved literally $1,000's with this advice.

Free Airfare Summary

The most expensive part of a Camino trip for most non-Europeans is the plane fare. Have you been thinking there is no getting around that expense? Think again! Let us introduce you to "travel-hacking" your way to Spain using frequent flyer miles earned from opening accounts with credit card companies offering 50,000-60,000 mile points with a new account when a certain spending requirement is met. First, let us set your mind at rest that everything we are going to tell you is perfectly legal and lets you as the consumer get the most out of some generous offers from credit card companies. Second, we do NOT suggest that people who are in debt, or struggle with staying out of debt get credit cards and use them to buy things on credit they cannot afford to pay for outright. What we are suggesting is that by opening accounts with one or two credit card companies, and using these cards for expenses you would be paying anyway, you can have enough frequent flyer miles to buy a round trip ticket from North America to Spain, and pay only the tax and airport fees. Our team members and readers have done this, and we hope that other countries will have something similar for those who do not reside in the U.S.

Here are our top recommendations for credit cards that will earn you free air fare: the Chase Sapphire Preferred Card, and the Citi Advantage Card. Plus, these cards do not charge foreign transaction fees if you use them internationally. With some creative thinking about your purchases using these cards, you can earn enough miles or points to exchange for a round trip ticket to Spain. Investigate your preferred departure airport to determine what airlines have the most flights, since different cards usually favor one airline over another. See details in **"Free Airfare STEP by STEP."**

Credit Cards, ATMs, & Cash

Spanish merchants and businesses prefer customers paying with a credit card to have a card that contains a chip, because their technology works best with this type. Many places cannot accept a card without a chip. Both the Chase Sapphire Preferred and the Citi Advantage are good choices for this reason, as both have chips. Spanish merchants prefer Visa and Mastercard, as the fees are lower than American Express, and many don't even accept Amex for this reason. It is rare that you cannot pay with your credit card, but you will still need to carry some cash. Some small cafés and markets, *albergues*, and local buses only accept cash.

Your best option for using the ATM (*Cajero Automático, or Telebanco*) is to bring to Spain the debit/ATM card associated with your checking account back home. Occasional withdrawals from your account via an ATM might not add up to much. If you withdraw 100€ at an ATM at the beginning of your trip, and use cash only when you cannot use your credit card, it may last the whole trip. However, if you want to consider opening an account that pays for all your international ATM fees as a perk, then look into an account with a company like Charles Schwab. Be sure to have some cash with you all the time, as there may not be an ATM when you need it. Be sure to have at least some of your cash in small denominations. You will need it most often for very small purchases like snacks or bus fare.

Daily Expenses

You can economize on your daily expenses if you are on a very tight budget by staying in municipal *albergues* and preparing your own food, living simply as you walk. Personalize your choices for your journey. For the more adventurous, around 30-40€ per day will allow you to stay in cheaper private *albergues* and an occasional hotel, eating simple meals and a daily pilgrim menu at a cafe or restaurant. If you can spend more the options are endless.

Student, Senior, and *Peregrino* Discounts

If you qualify to have an International Student Identity Card, be sure to have your current ISIC with you to receive student discounts on entrance fees along the Camino, and for other travel. You may find out more about ISIC at www.ISIC.org. Allow 3-4 weeks to apply and receive your card prior to use.

Senior citizens may purchase a discount card for rail service called the *Tarjeta Dorada* (which is good for one year) and gives you a 40% discount on Monday through Thursday travel, and 25% off Friday through Sunday travel. You must be at least 60 to be eligible for the "Gold Card," and you may purchase it for around 6€ at Renfe stations, ticket offices, and travel agencies. Some bus lines offer senior discounts for 60+, and our advice is to ask as you buy your ticket.

Seniors 65 and older do receive discounts at most museums. Look for the Spanish words *mayor discuenta*, which indicates a senior discount.

It is a good idea in general to ask what discounts might apply when purchasing tickets or paying admission fees to museums and some cathedrals. Along the Camino routes showing your pilgrim *credenciál* often gives you a significant discount on admission fees, and qualifies you to stay at the municipal albergues that are the cheapest.

Prepare

We are giving you the best information our team has to help you prepare for a successful walk on the Camino de Santiago. We have been in many gatherings of returning pilgrims in the U.S. in which at least one person dominates the conversation with tales of all the mishaps, bad weather, and strain they encountered on their walk. It reminds us of the people who like to tell their labor and delivery horror stories to pregnant couples. We are giving you the information that will enable you to make decisions and choices that are right for you as you plan, knowing that you will revise and fine tune what you do as you gain experience. Even well-intended returning pilgrims may give you impressions that will create fear. Our message to you is, Do not fret, all will be well.

Take Care of Yourself Before You Go

Make sure you are in good health for the walk. Your visits to the dentist and doctor should be up-to-date. Talk with your doctor about going on this journey to make sure he agrees that you are healthy enough to do it. Take good care of yourself while you are walking. Download a free copy of <u>Camino First Aid</u>, from our website, and read through it as a worthy reference about preventing and treating the most common injuries on the Camino. You will be entertained and informed by the authors, Tom and Em Hill, and because it is digital, you can have it with you in your e-library on your smart phone to use as a handy reference if you need help along the way. It is full of great Camino advice and excellent first aid guidance with diagrams. They help you diagnose injuries, tell you ways to treat them, and tell you how to determine when it is time to seek professional help from local medical personnel.

Physical Training

Being active and fit for your everyday life at home is good practice all the time, and it will help you accomplish the physical part of your Camino walk. So if you are not a very active person, begin taking steps to be active. Find ways to add activity to your day. The sooner you begin this, the better for your overall health *and* your upcoming Camino walk. The more you can walk as part of your every day life at home, the more you will learn what your capabilities are and determine what your pace and schedule might be on the Camino. We know an Olympic athlete who pushed herself to tears and minor injuries trying to cross the Pyrenees too fast, so even elite athletes need to determine their Camino pace and sustainability.

Try our recommendation to find your walking pace, **"How Long Will It Take Me?"**. The Camino experience is a day after day physical walk at its core. You need to set your own pace, and schedule time to rest and recover as you have need. If you fall behind the itinerary you set for yourself, rather than pushing yourself to injury by walking farther and faster than you should, hop a bus (cheap) or call a taxi to skip ahead. This may hurt your pride, but it is better to do this than have to quit and not finish like some of our family and friends who have suffered injuries from pushing too hard and carrying too much weight.

As soon as you can find and buy your footwear, walking poles, and backpack, start testing them out on walks where you live. Add weight to your pack slowly to build up strength and endurance. Attend to any hotspots on your feet from your new shoes, either by returning the shoes for a different pair, trying a different sock or insole, or applying Teflon pads, to the inside of your shoe at points of friction. Gradually increase walking to longer distances when you feel able, and discover your walking limits and recovery time. This will help you know how to pace yourself on the Camino in order to prevent overuse injuries, one of the most common reasons why people have to stop walking prematurely. Road test everything on several training hikes in plenty of time to make changes before your departure. Details in **"Favorite Gear,"** or **"Favorite Clothing & Footwear."**

Learn a Little Spanish

The most common language used along the Camino is English, but it is a nice gesture to learn how to say a few things to the residents along the Camino, and helpful to you as well. Speak Spanish as best as you can with a smile, and that will go a long way to show you are trying to honor them. Our favorite free app to help you with this, is the Duolingo app. You will hear many languages on the Camino. In fact on our first trip we stopped counting at 17. Group interaction at pilgrim gatherings and meals often goes like this: A native French speaker says something in French to an Italian, who speaks French and English, and the Italian translates into English, while a native

German speaker, who speaks English and French, translates the re-sponse back into French! It is great fun and all part of the community experience on the Camino. Another helpful tool is a translation app when you have internet available. Download the free **Google Trans-late app** from iTunes **or** Google Play onto your smart phone as a helpful interpretation aid. The app lets you type or write on your touch screen, or speak words to be translated. You can read or listen to the translation. Also, you can point at text with your phone's cam-era to have it translated. It has worked well translating into Spanish from English, and the other way around. Pretty amazing.

Order Your Pilgrim Passport (*Credenciál*)

You may order this ahead of time from American Pilgrims on the Camino (APOC), and other online pilgrim resources (allow 4-6 weeks). Go to APOC's Credential Request page for details: https://americanpilgrims.org/request-a-credential/. See the **"Re-Entry"** chapter for other pilgrim resources.

You may also buy a *credenciál* when you arrive at the Pilgrim Of-fice in St. Jean Pied-de-Port during office hours, and at churches or some albergues in other towns along the Camino. It saves a bit of time and stress to get it ahead of time in case the Pilgrim Office is closed when you need to buy it. The *credenciál* allows you certain privileges, and the only requirement for being a pilgrim is that you walk, ride a bicycle or horse, or roll in a wheelchair. You will have to show it at public albergues to qualify to sleep there that night, and you must get your *credenciál* stamped each day at your alber-gue or hotel in order to qualify to stay at the next town's municipal albergue. The cost to stay in a municipal albergue, or refugio, is usually 3-5€, but there are still a few designated as *donativo* (do-nate what you are able).

Beds at municipal albergues are given on a first come, first served basis, with priority given to ill or injured pilgrims, then pilgrims on foot carrying their backpacks, then pilgrims on bikes, horse or donkey, then pilgrims with luggage transported by a vehicle. If there are no beds left, some hosts *(hospitaleros)* offer a thin mat for a spot of floor on an outside porch, or will refer you to another option.

As mentioned earlier, many towns also have hotels or pensions of varying costs, or perhaps there might be a room in a private home available. In cities you might find a rental through a company like AirBnB.

In Santiago, it is your *credenciál* with its *sellos* (stamps) that proves you have earned your *compostela*. You must prove with your *credenciál* that you have walked a minimum of the final 100km or cycled the last 200km. You may get a stamp at any albergue, hotel, and church you pass during open hours on the Camino. Your *credenciál* also qualifies you to eat free at the humble Pilgrim's meal at the upscale Parador Hotel in Santiago. The hotel feeds the first ten credentialed pilgrims who are in line, though it is not in their fancy dining room. Other privileges afforded peregrinos with a *credenciál* include discounted entrance fees at museums and cathedrals on the Camino routes.

Other Necessary Documents

If you are a citizen of a country outside the European Union traveling to Spain, you will need a valid passport from your home country, which will allow you to stay in Spain as a tourist for up to 90 days. Most travelers coming from English-speaking countries do not need a visa, but you can check this online for the current status. Not only do you need a passport, but you need to make sure it will not expire for six months after your return date, and that it has enough empty pages for your trip. Each country's immigration service you plan to visit on your trip may want a page for itself, plus a page for the one you will receive when you return to your home country. It is a good idea to scan or photograph the profile pages of your passport and have this information accessible digitally in cyber storage (like <u>Dropbox</u>) or in your phone's photo library in case of loss or theft. The same goes for credit card account numbers and the toll free phone numbers used to report a missing card, and any other important information you can digitize and access if needed.

Buy Travel Medical Insurance

We recommend getting travel medical insurance that includes coverage for the travel expenses connected to medical treatment, plus coverage for treatment for illness while you are traveling internationally. Minor medical treatments are not expensive in Spain if you elect not to buy insurance, but our advice is to have it. Non-EU citizens must be prepared to cover clinic and hospital bills. Our team members have used plans from <u>International Medical Group</u>. Another company favored by many travelers is <u>World Nomads</u>.

Receiving a Pilgrim Blessing Before You Leave Home

Many churches will offer a blessing to those setting out on pilgrimage; just ask your local church, pastor, or priest. What if you're not a Christian? You can still receive a blessing at a pilgrim's service, or ask some close friends or family members to join you for a send off meal where they toast you with their well wishes for your journey.

Favorite Gear

Key points to remember about what you take with you:

- We have never met a pilgrim who wished he was carrying more gear.

- We have met many, many, many pilgrims who wished they were carrying less.

- We have interviewed lots of seasoned pilgrims, and spent lots of cash trying out clothes and gear to road test for ourselves and for you in order to present our favorite items to you We have sifted through lots of gravel to find the gems. We do Not recommend any item we do not have in our Camino backpack. You're welcome!

W e continue to test and review gear, and will post any good finds on our FaceBook page @CaminoProvisions, and on our "Gear Reviews" tab on our website, Camino-Provisions.com.

Backpacks

The elements we have found to be most important are correct size for your gear, front access in addition to top access, proper fit, lightweight yet durable fabric, built in rain cover, and plenty of pockets inside and out, some with zippers for security. The size pack you need will depend on the time of year you walk. If the weather is cold, you may need more room for the bulkier gear and clothing you will need to stay warm, while summer allows a more streamlined pack. Also important to those traveling by plane to begin the Camino is for your pack to fit in the overhead bin so you don't chance having it misplaced in the baggage handling process.

Use your torso length to find your best fit in a backpack. To do this, ask a friend to use a tape measure to find your torso length: Stand tall, bend your head down to look at your feet, making it easier to find your C7 vertebra, which is the bony bump at the base of your neck. This is the top of your torso. To find the bottom of your torso, rest your hands on your your iliac crest, the top of your hip bones, with your thumbs pointing back and your fingers pointing forward. The midpoint between your thumbs is the bottom of your torso. Use this measurement to find your best pack size. Look for these sizes on the tag at the store, or in the online sizing description.

- Up to 15"=Extra Small

- 16-17.5"=Small

- 18-19.5"=Medium/ Regular

- 20" and up=Large/Tall

Our favorites are from the Deuter family of packs: the *ACT Trail 28SL* or *ACT Trail Pro 32SL*, the *ACT Trail 30L,* or the *ACT Trail Pro 40L.* The 28SL and Pro 32SL are designed for shorter torsos, and have women-specific contoured front straps. The 30L and Pro 40L have all the great features of the others plus offer sizing for longer torsos, but do not have the women-specific straps. Any one of these four packs fits easily in the overhead bin on airplanes, so you don't take the chance of having it misplaced by checking it as baggage, and holds all the gear we recommend for your trip. Our favorite features are the front access panel (it also has a top access), its great pockets and straps, mesh hip belt and other ventilation features, and its built in rain cover. Here is a link to a good video about how to properly adjust your pack, www.youtube.com/watch?v=R-jGvGYpz2s.

Whether you choose the Deuter or something else, it is handy to pack a small tote bag for carrying shopping and laundry, allowing you to stow or consign your big pack while you do these errands. A bag we like is the *Baggu Reusable Shopping Bag.* It is made of ripstop nylon, holds up to 50 pounds, folds into a tiny pouch, weighs less than 1 ounce and comes in an array of colors and patterns.

Walking Poles

If you have never used walking poles, it may be hard to imagine what a difference they make. Our family and most pilgrims highly recommend them. Here are the features to look for when shopping: lightweight, durable, adjustability for perfect fit and travel, cork hand grip, carbide tips for dirt/rock paths plus optional rubber feet for walking on pavement, and detachable hand straps. Search for "walking poles," or "Nordic walking poles," rather than "trekking poles." You will hear pilgrims refer to their poles as trekking poles even when they may technically be labeled walking poles. Our recommendation is *Leki Traveller Carbon Nordic*

Walking Poles, and the less expensive *Leki Traveler Aluminum.* The pair of Carbon Travelers weigh in at 14.6 oz. (the Aluminum set is 16.6oz.).

While we have not been stopped from carrying our walking poles stowed in our backpacks onto a plane in the USA, the official word from TSA is that they are not allowed in a carry-on bag, but only as checked baggage. Our current solution to this challenge is to get a free USPS *priority mail medium tube*, insert our collapsed poles, mark well inside and out with our name and address, tape closed, and check when we fly. In the last four years, we have always had to check the poles as baggage on the return home flights. We discard the box responsibly upon arrival, and begin using the poles, or affix them to the outside of our packs. We also take an extra pair of the rubber feet on our Camino journeys. We have used *Stansport Trekking Pole Replacement Feet (2 Pack)*, and like them for less than half the price of Leki brand rubber replacement feet. On the flight home we use our weightless Baggu tote bags as carry-ons along with a shopping bag with any snacks, and check our backpacks with our poles in them as baggage.

Why use poles? This is an excellent question. When they are adjusted to the right size for your height, and used properly poles will redistribute some of the workload of walking from your legs to your arms and torso, thereby literally taking some of the load off of your ankles, knees, hips and leg muscles, and engaging your arm, shoulder, and back muscles to help with the work. They give you better balance on all types of terrain. We have discussed many times how glad we all were to have poles to help us on many, many sections of the trail. Even some simpler ascents and descents can become dangerous when wet from fog and rain. If you should ever need to fend off a dog or other animal, a walking pole is a handy extension to your arm to keep a safe distance as you walk on by.

What is the difference between trekking poles and walking poles? From our research the biggest difference is the handgrip and strap design. Most of the path on the Camino de Santiago is on groomed dirt/rock trails and a variety of pavements, so it will benefit you to put the walking style poles to work for you. The hand straps on the walking poles allow a very natural walking motion and because the strap is fit to your hand with a Velcro closure, the straps comfortably pull the pole into place for your next step without chafing your hand. With the style of hand strap on the trekking poles we have discovered a need to grasp the grip more tightly to bring the pole into place, with the straps rubbing our hands more. When encountering more uneven terrain, the walking poles provide plenty of support and balance with their carbide tips helping to keep your footing. The rubber feet are an important option for gripping hard surfaces safely, and also muffling the metal tips' "klick klack, klick klack" sound for yourself and everyone around you.

Sleeping Bags

Check online to discover the temperature ranges you can expect for the time of year you will be walking. Choose the most compact bag with a warmth rating appropriate to these temperatures. Keep in mind that elevation affects temperatures, too, with cooler temperatures at higher altitudes like the Pyrenees and O'Cebreiro.

If you want an excellent three-season sleeping bag our favorite is the **Marmot Trestles 30**. Lightweight, compact, and super efficient. Perfect for Camino use. Our favorite warm weather sleeping system is the **Sea to Summit Adapter Liner with Insect Shield**. Sleep inside or on top, add an albergue blanket or not. Layer your clothes if you need more warmth for a night or two.

Most private albergues and hotels provide sheets and blankets on their beds, so you will not need to bring your own sleeping gear if you are planning on using these types of accommodations every night. Nevertheless, we recommend taking the Sea to Summit

Adaptor Liner with Insect Shield so that you can sleep in it if needed, or use it in conjunction with hotel bedding.

Pillow

Some albergues and all hotels have pillows on their beds. If you can't imagine traveling for a month without your own pillow, then here is our recommendation. We favor stuffing soft clothes in our sleeping bag storage sack to serve as a pillow, but if that just won't do it for you, consider the *Sea to Summit Aeros Pillow ultra light.* Decide whether the comfort a pillow provides is worth carrying the extra weight. One of your soft tee shirts can double as a pillowcase.

Earplugs

You may not have had much luck with earplugs in the past because you were using the ones they give away free on airplanes, but earplugs that actually work and are comfortable may become your best friends on the Camino. They might be your best defense against some of the most annoying, sleep-depriving creatures along the Camino—The "snore-a-dores." When you are trying to sleep in a communal situation like an albergue or airplane, *Mack's Ultra Soft Foam Earplugs* can help you get the sleep you need. "These ear plugs are molded with super low-pressure, skinned and tapered foam to provide unmatched comfort and improved hygiene. With a high noise reduction rating (NRR) of 32 decibels, this high performance hearing protection can be used in environments where noise is just a nuisance up to environments with hazardous noise levels." The jar we suggest you buy here is less than $9 for 50 pairs. The whole jar weighs less than 4oz., and you only need to pack 5-10 pairs. Each pair gives you multiple uses, but you may lose one here or there.

Favorite Way to Carry Water

Specially designed hiker water bottles and bladders are nice, but we prefer to carry water in a 20-ounce plastic water/soda bottle purchased along the Camino. Use it for a couple days, refilling as necessary, then recycle that one and buy a new one. It is very hard to keep refillable water systems safely clean for 4-6 weeks on the Camino de Santiago, especially the ones with hoses that allow you to sip as you walk. A plastic soda bottle is also the most lightweight. This is very important because water is heavy! But if you don't drink enough water without having a tubing delivery system, consider the *Source Convertube Water Bottle Adaptor System*. It works with many water bottles including our 20 oz. recyclable ones.

Using Your Smart Phone to Its Best Advantage

While we hope you will consider taking a break from the demands of electronic communication and the life noise that can come through your phone, a smart phone is the one and only piece of technology we recommend for your trip on the Camino. In addition to giving you phone service for safety, information, and convenience purposes, your smart phone can multi-task to record your photos, provide a time keeping device, journal, and calendar. Use it to look up and book transportation and lodging, and provide handy amenities like a mirror or white noise to drown out "snore-a-dores" at albergues. Read more details in **"Best Phone Apps."** Be sure to pack your charging cable and an appropriate electrical outlet adapter for Spain with your phone.

Favorite Phone Service Plan

We highly recommend getting a service plan that provides inexpensive cellular service while traveling internationally. T-Mobile has what we think is the best plan for U.S. pilgrims, and we will update you on our FaceBook @CaminoProvisions page if this changes. Check it out online here www.t-mobile.com, or visit a T-Mobile store near you.

Second best? If your smart phone is unlocked, it is pretty easy to buy a Spanish SIM card to pop in and a "pay-as-you-go service plan" when you get to Pamplona. Not every town has a phone store to offer SIM cards, and each country requires a different SIM. Several providers dominate the Spanish cellular landscape: Vodafone, Orange, and Movistar are the most popular. Until you find a phone store you will have to submit to the super high prices of your provider's international cellular plan, or be content to use wifi-only communication (email and wifi calling) until you can get the SIM card. Also, see our list of **"Helpful Phone Numbers for Spain."**

Digitize Travel Documents and Important Information

Bring printed copies or digitized copies in cyber storage of the mailing addresses of friends and families you intend to contact while you are traveling, and copies of all your travel documents. Any digitized information kept on a smart phone should be protected with a strong password, and your phone kept secure at all times. If you are not using your cell phone, keep it stowed on your person and out of sight.

Favorite Phone Apps

We do want to recommend again that you limit your use of technology on the Camino in order to live in the present. But your phone can also provide safety and connectivity in helpful ways as you travel. Make the best use of your phone with some helpful travel apps.

Rome2Rio.com: Free app providing routing information between any two cities around the world, with mileage, what types of transportation is available, and links to bus, train, car, plane websites.

Booking.com: Free app for booking stays in hotels around the world. See availability, pricing, and locations quickly, and reserve your room.

AirBnB.com: Free app for booking stays in private homes, apartments, or whole houses around the world. Download the app free, create a profile, and shop for accommodations in your desired location. Reserve and pay online with your credit card.

GoogleTranslate.com: Free app is a helpful interpretation aid. The free version lets you type or handwrite on your touch screen, or speak words to be translated. You can read or listen to the translation. You can also take a picture of a sign or other text with your phone's camera to have it translated. It has worked well translating into Spanish from English, and the other way around. Google Translate app from iTunes or Google Play

Duolingo.com: Free downloadable interactive language instruction program

Keep Your Phone Dry!

Anyone who has been faced with trying to dry out a phone and rescue the data from it will already know the importance of having waterproof protection for your phone. This can be as simple as a tightly sealed zip-able, plastic food storage bag, or as sturdy as a waterproof case made for your phone. Our favorite solution is to have one x-small *Sea to Summit Lightweight Dry Sack*, that you will put your passport and other paper documents and valuables in, along with your phone if it starts raining.

Favorite Soaps and Lotions

Our favorite "wash everything soap" is *Camp Suds*, which can clean your body and hair, your clothes, and pretty much anything else. It has a pleasant mint fragrance and lathers well. It is available in several sizes, and we advise filling a ***GoToob*** (see next section) rather than using the bottle it comes in because the provided bottle top design is one that often opens and leaks in your pack. Our favorite safe sun protection products are from <u>BeautyCounter</u> and have an SPF 30. Choose lotion and fill a couple of 3oz GoToobs with it, or choose a solid/stick version. If you have to be very careful of sun exposure like some of us do, you might consider using a ***"Sun Buff."*** Fishermen have been using these for years, and they are another multi-use item for the Camino. This soft microfiber cloth cylinder can be pulled over your head to your neck, then pulled up as far as you need to cover the lower part of your face not protected by your hat, to provide complete sun block. It can also be worn as a hair band, ponytail scrunchy, around your neck like a scarf, or on your wrist for a pop of color. Colors and styles are practically endless, but I recommend checking out the Camino designs as a fun memento of your walk. More about SPF clothing in **"Favorite Clothing."**

Favorite Way to Transport Liquids

We have found nothing we like better than ***GoToobs*** for transporting liquid soaps and lotions. They come in three sizes, have a clever system of labeling what you put in them, and are easily refillable along your walk, allowing you to carry on TSA approved liquids as you fly, and replenishing along the Camino as needed. ***GoTubbs*** are also handy. They come in two sizes and are a great invention for transporting dry items like pills, or anything small you want to keep organized. Open with one hand and push to snap closed.

Towel

Our favorite towel for the Camino is the ***Packtowel Personal Travel Towel*** in size XL or XXL. It dries your body as well as any travel towel we have tried, dries quickly, is very small and light weight, and has a handy snapping loop on one corner which makes it easy to hang up somewhere to dry. It comes in a variety of colors, and we suggest choosing an easily identifiable color to distinguish your towel on community clotheslines.

The Pareo Option, More than a Towel

Ladies, it is hard to know whether to put this item on your clothing list or on the gear list, because it has so many uses. You might use a pareo instead of a towel, or as a bunk curtain for privacy, emergency swim pants, picnic blanket, skirt, shawl, or sun protection. Choose yours from many prints and patterns. Choose a lightweight natural or microfiber fabric for quick drying. Here is one in all cotton. We advise washing in cold water and hanging to dry to prevent shrinkage. Something like the **Anika Dali Claire Birds Scarf** has worked well, and is attractive.

Miscellaneous Little Gear

Here are a few items that didn't fit in another section, but will be valuable to you. Your smart phone can serve as a flashlight when you don't need both hands free, but our team recommends a headlamp for hands-free walking with poles, or just for reading in bed before lights out. The one we like for its weight, price and effectiveness is this **LED Headlamp**. Weighing in at a mere 2.6 ounces, this ultra lightweight headlamp has high beam, low beam and flashing settings, and runs off of 3 AAA batteries, which are included. TIP: If you ever find yourself walking in heavy fog, especially when the sun is not up, a headlamp worn on your forehead will reflect back off the fog and impede your visibility. So rather than wear it on your forehead, fasten it at your waist and direct the light beam at the ground to illuminate the path ahead.

Take a **Small Roll of Duct Tape** to mend your gear or use 1000 other ways. The handy size we like is listed on our website "Gear Reviews" tab, should serve you well for emergency repairs, and is not very heavy.

Take along a few **large safety pins**, the kind that are about 2" long, in one of your **GoTubbs**. These will come in handy for pinning up clothes and towels on your bunk to dry or provide privacy, fix broken straps, or take in the waistband of your pants if they get too baggy because you lose weight.

A **3X5" notebook** and pen come in handy for leaving notes for friends on message boards, and jotting notes when you hear about recommendations of where to eat or stay in the next town. We recommend using your smart phone to take notes and journal most everything, but sometimes it is super handy to have a little notebook and pen.

If you take our advice about having a smart phone with you, be sure to take an appropriate **electrical outlet adapter for Spain** if your charging cable is from the U.S.

Take a tiny sewing kit from a hotel stay, or take a needle and 2 feet of strong black thread wound around a 1"x2" piece of card stock. The safety pins and the needle and thread will easily fit into a small plastic medicine bottle or 2 oz **GoTubb** so they will be easy to find in your pack.

Favorite Clothing and Footwear

O ur clothing recommendations include items we think every *peregrino* needs, and we mention the features that make them our favorites. In general all of your clothing needs to be comfortable and wash-and-dry. We will update our favorites list on our website, and our FaceBook page. Sign up to receive our free emails, and like our FB page so you get all the latest news and reviews.

Your "Footwear System"

Your feet are carrying you the whole way so you need to get this right above all else. What you wear on your feet for your long daily walks can be looked at as a footwear system: your sock, your insole or orthotic, your shoes, and anti-chafing product. Not only do you need to choose comfort, but also support.

Trail Shoes

Because of the importance of your foot health to accomplish the mileage you will cover day after day, there is more discussion about footwear among future and veteran pilgrims than almost any other gear. Our teammates and family have tried on dozens and dozens of pairs, and walked the Camino with traditional hiking boots, lighter weight hiking shoes, and even hiking sandals.

Fit and features: your feet will naturally swell a bit after you have been walking for a couple hours, so try on trail shoes later in the day when your feet are their normal been-on-your-feet size. If you can possibly access a store with personnel trained in fitting hiking footwear, do it. We recommend a lightweight, waterproof hiking shoe, and our favorite is the ***Merrell Moab Gore-Tex Waterproof Hiking Shoe***. It comes in extended men's and women's sizing, and has all the features we have come to appreciate in our trail shoes. You will see a LOT of *peregrinos* wearing this shoe because of its support, comfort, and overall fit.

Socks

The features we like in a sock are good fit and wick-ability. You should not have any loose or bunching fabric that can wrinkle up and cause a friction point. Dry feet are much less likely to produce friction, which leads to blisters, so you want to choose a material that wicks moisture away from your skin. Our two favorites: one for people who like a thicker sock and one for those liking thinner socks. Our favorite thick sock is ***Fits***. They come in medium or lighter weight thickness crew socks, and a lightweight ankle high version ("Quarter"). They are the best fitting socks we have tested! For thin sock people, we love the **Wrightsock**--a great fitting, double layer, microfiber, and ankle high.

Insoles

The **Superfeet** Company makes several non-prescription insoles that can replace the insoles that come in your trail shoes to give you more support. They come in shoe sizes and a variety of support profiles, and can be customized easily with scissors to fit in your shoe perfectly. We like the green ones best for distances of up to 15 miles per day.

If you are over 40 or have chronically sore feet after long hikes, consider a visit to a reputable sports podiatrist for a consultation about ordering custom orthotics. These can be pricey, but insurance often covers the cost.

Anti-Chafing Lubricants

Many veteran peregrinos have used petroleum jelly to prevent chafing and blisters on feet, inner thighs, inside upper arms, etc. **Trail Toes** is a favorite of ultra marathoners, and it is now our favorite. It comes in a 2oz. jar, which should be the right amount for a month long Camino for one person, and weighs only 3oz. An honorable mention goes to **Glide**, which comes in a couple of sizes, in the form of a crank up "solid" similar to some deodorants. It is a bit easier to carry, but a bit more difficult to apply.

Blister Prevention & Treatment

We discovered our favorite blister prevention and treatment products back in 2007 before walking the Camino for the first time, and in the years since then these products have helped countless *peregrinos* go blister-free, or treat their blisters and keep walking. As you are breaking in your new hiking shoes, you may notice some hotspots where some part of your shoe is causing a spot on your foot to become hot and red. Think of this as a pre-blister. Make sure this does not indicate a shoe that does not fit. If it is just a matter of being a tenderfoot, or overdoing it, consider preventing further friction with a product called **Engo Blister Prevention Patches.** These adhesive-backed teflon patches attach to the parts of your shoes that are causing any hotspots, and stop the friction to allow the hotspot on your foot to heal rather than progress to a blister.

If you do get blisters, it will be good to treat them with **Spenco 2nd Skin Gels.** We have tried all the remedies and bandages on the market, even the European ones promoted everywhere, and the Spenco gels are our favorite. If you are walking the Camino solo, get one or two of the **Spenco 2nd Skin Blister Kits**, which are about $10 each, and contain some gel squares and knit adhesive tape to treat inflamed skin and blisters. Or, you might prefer to invest in the following two items in bulk, even though you may not need to take all of it with you. If you are walking with friends, share the cost of these two Spenco products to divide among you: a jar of 200 **Spenco 2nd Skin Gel Squares** and a box or two of **Spenco Adhesive Knit Sports** tape. Here's how it works: The gel squares are moist pads you put directly on your clean, damaged skin and hold in place with a piece of the tape placed over the gel pad. These not only bring immediate relief to your damaged skin, but provide a comfortable buffer allowing you to keep walking without doing more damage. This stuff is amazing!!! I cannot recommend these products highly enough.

After-Hours Shoes

Most peregrinos are very happy to put on their comfortable, supportive trail shoes in the morning, but are ready to take them off when they check-in to their albergue or hotel for the night. You need something else when you finish your walk every day, and since you are carrying it in your pack, it had better be weightless. Because it can get cool at night along the Camino except maybe in summer, we prefer something that can be worn with socks, but can also be worn without socks into the shower. Our favorites: for women—***Croc Cleo Slides*** and for men—***Croc Brava Slides.***

Sun Buffs

Sunburn is one of the most hazardous and painful injuries for *peregrinos.* In addition to taking precautions with the topical sun-screens already mentioned, wise peregrinos can prevent serious sunburns with their clothing. Two years ago a friend introduced us to **Buffs,** a soft microfiber cylindrical scarf that can provide protection from the elements for your face, neck, head. Buffs brand products come in a variety of colors and prints, and come in adult and children's sizes, as well as warm weather versions and winter versions. Wear your Buff around your neck, pull one end up to cover the part of your face not shaded by your hat, wear it as a headband or head covering, use it to hold a pony tail, or add a pop of color on your wrist. The original Buffs Company has even designed a **Buffs Camino Collection** which features nice designs for men and women in attractive and fun colors. Make this a memento of your trip.

Pants, Shorts, Skirts

Look for these features: Quick drying fabric, breathable, comfortable waistband adjustable with a belt or drawstring for a fluctuating waistline size; at least one secure pocket with zipper, Velcro or snap closure big enough for your cell phone and another for your wallet, passport and pilgrim *credenciál;* extra pockets for storing *panuelos* (tissues to use during toilet stops), or anything you might want to access easily during your walk without getting into your pack; pants legs may be worn full length for sun protection or rolled or gathered up for cooling off after your walk. Easy to hand wash and line dry. Choose colors that will be forgiving of dirt and stains. Two pairs. If you decide to wear long pants for your walk and shorts or skirt for after hours, you could get by with two items, but do choose at least one long option for sun protection.

Ladies, our Camino favorite pant is the **Columbia Saturday Trail Pant**. We also like the **Royal Robbins Discovery Skirt** rather than shorts because it is cooler. It could even be worn with leggings if the weather is cool. By the way, leggings are a useful clothing item for the Camino as they can be worn for sleeping or after hours with a pareo wrapped as a skirt, or on the trail with a Discovery Skirt for full sun protection. *Peregrinas* who have tried a skirt for their walking clothing like them especially for the modesty a skirt provides when answering calls of nature along the trail. Our favorite leggings are **Columbia Luminary Leggings,** which can easily be worn alone, and even have a decent pocket with a zipper for your phone or passport. Men, we like the **Columbia Silver Ridge Cargo Pant or Shorts.** Great fit, pockets, and weight for the Camino.

Shirts, Blouses, Tops

Look for these features: Quick drying, breathable fabric, long sleeves that can roll up for after hours, sun blocking, and wrinkle-free. You will want quick-drying fabric because you will be able to wash it out at the end of every day you wear it, and it will be dry to wear or pack the next morning. Breathable fabric is best, because chances are you will be walking when it is warm, and you won't want your clothing to make you hot and sweaty. Long sleeves and sun blocking fabric are a good idea, because you need to protect yourself from sunburn, and wrinkle-free, because why not look fresh instead of a mess? Good pockets are also a plus, but not necessary if you have good pockets in your pants and are carrying your pack.

A lot of tops out there offer a couple of these features, but our favorites have them all, plus have features that double their function and include some style. ***Columbia Button-up Collared Shirts for Men***, and ***Columbia Blouses for Women*** come in a variety of colors and patterns. They are made from a quick drying, breathable, sun blocking, wrinkle resistant fabric and have convertible long sleeves that roll up and button into a short sleeve. The sleeves also feature a cuff design that covers more of the top of your hand, an especially nice feature when walking in the sun on the Camino, and the two-button adjustment on the cuff gives you a good fit. The collar can flip up to offer sun protection for your neck, and two zippered breast pockets can serve to keep small valuables safe. Columbia also makes long sleeved pullover knit shirts in an amazing fabric they call Omni-freeze. It has a special texture built into the fabric that actually accentuates evaporative cooling when you begin to perspire, and keeps you cooler. We have tested these shirts and can tell the difference. They are sun blocking and wrinkle free, come in several neck styles and colors, and are very comfy worn alone, as a base layer under another top, or to sleep in. ***Columbia Omni Freeze Knit Shirts for Men*** and ***Columbia Omni-Freeze Knit Shirts for Women***. Even if you typically choose a v-neck for casual wear at home, remember a v-neck on the Camino means you have to wear a bandana or sunscreen to protect what is not covered by the shirt. Columbia also makes a ***Women's Tank Top*** with a wide enough strap to wear a bra with, and it works well as a base layer, sleepwear, or after hours blouse for warm weather. A tank top does not offer enough sun protection for your long daily walk, but it can come in handy to layer and vary your outfit for after hours, or sleeping.

Bandana

A 23"x23" bandana is handy for *peregrinos*. Use it around your neck to warm up your whole body. Protect your head or neck from sunburn. Tie on a flighty hat on a windy day. Control long hair in the wind. Soak in cool water or wrap up some ice and tie loosely around your neck to help cool your body on a hot day with an evaporative cooling effect. Folded once to make a triangle, it can be tied loosely around your neck to be pulled up cowboy style over your mouth and nose when the wind is kicking up a lot of dust. We use bandanas when walking past dry fields being plowed for planting, or for filtering car and truck fumes along busy roads. It can also be used as part of a makeshift bandage system in an emergency. Use it to carry dry snacks by placing the snacks in the center, gathering up the four corners and tying them off as snug as needed to secure your snack. And of course it can add a note of your personal style when tied on yourself or your pack. Choose a quick-drying fabric, either microfiber or silk, as you will want to rinse or wash this out frequently. We like ***ExOfficio Bugsaway Paisley Bandana.*** It comes in nice colors, has a UPF of 30, and built in insect repellent effective against mosquitoes (including those carrying West Nile virus and malaria), ticks, ants, flies, chiggers, midges, and no-see-ums. The Insect Shield lasts for 70 washings.

Hat

Look for these features: broad brim all the way around the head, washable, quick-drying fabric, stow-able chin string, ventilated. Two of the most serious and common injuries on the Camino are foot blisters and sunburns. A bad sunburn is very dangerous, not only because of the damage and discomfort to your skin, but if serious enough, it can affect your liver. That is why we keep emphasizing protecting yourself with clothing items and lotion sunscreens. Not only is a hat important for sun protection of your face and neck, but it also can provide a cooling effect for your head on long sunny stretches of trail. A broad brim all around gives the best shade. A baseball style cap makes a nice fashion accessory, but it doesn't do the whole job your trail hat needs to do. A washable, quick-drying fabric is a must because, well, it's going to get really sweaty, and you will get rained on, and you might want to rinse it off and have it dry to wear a few hours later. We prefer a chinstrap or string because the winds can get fierce on many stretches of the Camino, and you have to be able to keep it on. When not needed, tuck the string away.

Our favorite hat is a Tilley. Hands down. This Canadian company guarantees their hats for life against failure, will return a found hat to its registered owner, and has a big range of sizes and pleasing colors. A variety of styles offer mesh fabric in the crown of the hat to allow more air circulation to increase the evaporative cooling effect on your head. It is an expensive first time investment, but a Tilley is guaranteed to last you a lifetime. Some people personalize their Tilleys with mementoes from their travels like pins and patches.

Underwear

Look for these features: Quick-drying fabric, good fit (no wrinkles to cause friction blisters), good support, comfortable waist bands on briefs, comfortable bands and straps on bras.

Ladies

Walking is a low impact exercise, so you do not need to wear a super bounce-proof sports bra on the Camino. Whatever choice will be the most supportive and comfortable bra for you to wear walking at home is what you should wear on the Camino. In our research, we have talked with many *peregrinas* and have tried different kinds, and the women on our team are most comfortable in a regular bra made of quick drying fabric that fits great and looks great under clothes. Try out your selection on your training hikes when you test equipment for hours of walking to determine whether there are any friction points that cause chafing. I recommend taking two bras. If you can't wear the ones you usually wear for some reason, our team picks something like *Patagonia Barely Bra* as our favorite with an honorable mention going to *Jockey Micro Seamfree Cami Strap Bralette*.

While ExOfficio underwear comes highly recommended at some outdoor stores, we found the elastic they use on their waist bands to be a bit thick and uncomfortable, especially under your pack's hip belt. Also, with many people using this brand, people often have the same style and color, and I have known several people who had theirs mistakenly taken by someone else from the clothes lines at albergues. We like something like **Patagonia Active Briefs** from REI because they are seamless, so there's no chafing, and they have a wide, flat, soft waistband that doesn't dig into your skin like the other brands do. They come in several fun colors that are easy to spot on the albergue clothesline, but won't need to be there long because they dry so quickly. We recommend taking three pairs of briefs.

Consider taking a small supply of panty liners to provide a freshening up which can lengthen the time you can wear a pair of briefs.

Guys

The same features that women look for are what guys should be looking for in their briefs--quick drying, good fitting, and supportive. Walking the Camino may be low impact, but it is a strenuous, athletic endeavor, and your choice of briefs should reflect that. A sports style brief like **ExOfficio Give-n-Go Boxer Brief** is the favorite of the men on our team. Test your choice on long hikes to make sure they work without chafing.

Jacket

Look for these features in a three-season jacket: Lightweight, waterproof and windproof, integrated hood that can be rolled up into the collar out of your way when you don't need it, breathability, pit zips and venting, good pockets, velcro-cinch cuffs on the sleeves, adjustable drawstring at the bottom hem, Velcro AND a zipper front closure placket. Great colors are a bonus. Our team's favorite jacket for men and women is the **Marmot Precip Jacket**. It has all of the features we want in a three-season waterproof jacket, and fits so that there is room to wear a fleece or warm layer under it for cooler temperatures in spring and fall. When you don't have it on this jacket can fold into one of its pockets, or can be tied to the outside of your pack to dry. It is available in many colors and has a lifetime warranty. You will get your money's worth. It's our top pick for a three season Camino jacket.

Favorite Rain Solution

In addition to your Marmot Precip, you will need a waterproof pack cover, if your pack doesn't have one built in. Our favorite is the *Sea to Summit Ultra-Light Cordura Pack Cover.* It is made of Siliconized Cordura nylon for durability and waterproofing, is super lightweight at 3oz., and stows away in its attached sack. Choose from several colors and sizes. We like the fact that there are no seams to leak, and the elastic adjusting cord is well designed to tighten around your pack. Even with a good pack cover and rain gear, we strongly advise you to protect all the contents of your pack and stay organized in waterproof packing cubes. We like the *Eagle Creek Packing Cubes* in white. These super lightweight, zip-closure cubes are made of water repellant ripstop fabric to help keep water out, organize your stuff, and make loading your pack simpler. If you dropped one in the bathtub, it would not keep out every drop of water, but as another barrier against rain on the Camino, they are perfect. The sets come in some fun colors, but we prefer white so that we can see what is inside the cube. You can also use Ziplock style food bags, but they are not sturdy enough to last for more than a couple of weeks.

Our recommendation is to carry one small completely waterproof bag to protect your phone, passport and other paper documents, medicine, and any other small item you have to keep absolutely bone dry. Our tried-and-true recommendation is the *Sea to Summit Lightweight Dry Sack* in the XS or even XXS size. These roll-down-and-clip shut sacks are made for kayakers, fishermen, and backpackers who need to keep gear dry. Very lightweight, affordable and well designed.

We also recommend rain gaiters to wear with your trail shoes or boots to keep the rain from running down into your footwear. If you have chosen our favorite trail shoes, the Merrell Moab waterproof, rain gaiters can be a brilliant addition to keep your feet drier in hard rain. We like *Docooler® Outdoor Waterproof Windproof Gaiters*. A pair costs less than $8 through our website, and they weigh less than 5 ounces. They have worked great for us on our Caminos during rain, and are good at keeping small pebbles out of our shoes when it isn't raining. They can also provide a layer of protection against cold wind in spring and fall trips. Wear over long pants or with shorts.

If the rain turns from a light drizzle to a downpour or starts coming at you sideways with some wind, we recommend having a 4-pack of plastic *Emergency Ponchos* handy. We have used these to good effect in many rainstorms recently. If you are careful one will serve you for several days' use, and they are super cheap and lightweight—about one ounce each. One poncho easily fits in a jacket pocket to be ready when you need it. Put on your precip jacket with its hood up, then your pack with its rain cover on, then put the poncho on with its hood over the precip hood, and then put your hat on. The poncho goes over you and your pack for an extra barrier against the rain. These particular ponchos are not as tent-like and billowy as some of the sturdier, re-useable side-snap variety, so they will not billow up as much when the wind gusts. If your pack is larger than our recommended size, these ponchos might not work for you, but they are a terrific solution for the rest of us. If you run out of the ones you bring with you, they are often available at shops along the Camino.

Sunglasses

A pair of polarized sunglasses is more than a fashion accessory on the Camino, it's one piece in your overall sun protection plan. A wrap around style is a good choice because so much of the time you are walking west and the sun is coming at you from the right or left. If you wear prescription eye glasses, consider a pair of the **Duco sunglasses**. There are many styles and colors from which to choose, and they are a good price point at around $25. If you don't wear eyeglasses, we love these **Flying Fisherman** brand sunnies. The prices are economical at around $13, and the range of colors and styles varied.

Top Travel Tips

Discounts? How to get around? FREE Airfare?! We are not kidding about this. We have paid full price on more than one Camino trip in the past, and we like flying for free much better! Many of our readers in the USA have joined us in saving BIG $$$$ with our tips to get free fare. Read on for all the insider tips on travel.

How to Get from Here to There

Getting around Spain and France to get to the city that will be your starting point can be daunting. The Rome2Rio website and app are free, and are great resources to find out how to get from any

"Point A" to any "Point B" in the world. Plug in a departure city and destination city and get options for traveling from one to the other—buses, trains, airplanes, and cars— and see links and estimated costs for each option.

Free Airfare

Getting to Spain or France to begin your Camino is one of the most expensive parts of your experience, particularly for Western Hemisphere residents. It can be the initial big hurdle people have to overcome before they can plan their Caminos. The cost for round trip air travel from North America averages around $1200 over the course of the year, making it prohibitive for some, and difficult for many future *peregrinos*.

What we propose as a way of not paying money for airfare involves absolutely legal "travel hacking" tips we have learned. Major airlines in the USA offer flight bookings in exchange for sky miles or travel points. 'Yes,' you say, 'but I don't have those kinds of sky miles built up, so that won't work for me.' Ah yes, but traveling by air is just one way of collecting sky miles. Here is how we and our readers get round trip tickets to Europe, paying only tax and airport fees, with some planning and effort a couple of months ahead.

As an incentive for opening a credit card account several companies offer LOTS of sky miles/points that you can redeem for airline tickets and other goods. Our favorite credit card deals now are listed here, but for the most up-to-date info, follow us on FaceBook (@CaminoProvisions) where we post updates on good deals we find.

A round trip flight to Europe in peak summer from the U.S. costs 60,000 miles. By receiving sign up bonus miles plus earning a few thousand more by using the card for a couple of months, we had more than enough miles to exchange for our flight to begin our Camino walk.

We are not suggesting that someone who has existing credit card debt, or who struggles with purchasing items on credit that he cannot afford should do this. A healthy use of credit cards to earn rewards is just good business when you use the cards only to charge those things which you can pay off as soon as the bill comes.

If you think this might be your ticket to Spain to walk the Camino, keep reading our step-by-step guide to free airfare.

STEP-BY-STEP: Free Airline Tickets

Begin these steps 6-12 months before your Camino travel dates.

Our two favorite USA airlines providing international service with frequent flyer mile tickets are United and American. Changes will appear in our FaceBook posts. You may have access to these airlines and already have a favorite, but if you don't then you might consider choosing the airline with the most flights from your departure airport. You might also look at out-of-pocket fees you will pay aside from "buying" the actual airfare with points/miles. The fuel surcharge, and other fees can vary greatly from airline to airline. British Airways charges notoriously high fuel charges, for instance.

If getting multiple cards will be a problem for you, determine which airline you will likely use based upon your location and home airport, i.e., United, American, or Delta. If you can use any airline, go for the Chase card as the Chase Ultimate Rewards points provide more flexibility.

Our favorite card for buying United Airlines tickets with miles is the ***Chase Sapphire Preferred*** credit card. A flight to Spain or France to begin walking the Camino will generally cost 60,000 Ultimate Rewards Points converted to United airfare. Chase also has agreements with Iberia and Virgin Atlantic Airlines, which fly to Europe. Set it up like this:

- Apply for the Chase Sapphire Preferred card. When you are approved just use your card to begin paying for your normal expenses and gift items.

- After spending $4,000 in 3 months with your new card, you earn a one-time bonus up to 60,000 (generally 50,000) Chase Ultimate Rewards points

- Then earn 10,000 more points any of the following ways:

  - Earn up to 10 points per dollar spent shopping through the Chase Shopping portal at hundreds of your favorite stores;

  - Earn 2 points per dollar spent for travel and dining;

  - Earn 1 point per dollar spent on everything else;

  - Earn 5,000 points for referring a friend who opens an account and uses their card.

- If you do not already have a United Mileage Plus account (their frequent flyer account) to accumulate miles/points from United Airlines, open one for free on their website.

- Once you have accumulated 60,000 Chase Ultimate Rewards points, go on the United website to check flight availability for the dates you can fly. The farther out you check, the more available rewards seats there will be.

- If there are available seats for rewards passengers, transfer just the necessary points to your United Mileage Plus account. They transfer 1:1 points to miles. Once you have transferred your points to your Mileage Plus Account, they stay there until used to pay for a flight.

- If you decide to use your Chase Ultimate Reward Points with Iberia or Virgin Atlantic, the process is similar to that with United.

The Chase card is also a good one to use to make purchases during your Camino trip since there is no foreign transaction fee charged, and the typical annual card fee of $95 is waived for the first year.

Our favorite card for buying American Airlines tickets with miles is the ***Citi AAdvantage Platinum Select Mastercard***. During peak travel months 60,000 miles will get you a round trip ticket from the USA to Spain.

- Open an American Airlines AAdvantage Rewards account if you don't already have one.

- Apply for the Citi AAdvantage Platinum Select Mastercard. When you are approved use your card to begin paying for your normal expenses and gift items.

- After spending $3,000 in the first 3 months after opening your MasterCard account, you earn a one-time bonus of up to 60,000 (generally 50,000) AAdvantage Reward Miles, so if you decide to fly before March or after November, you have enough miles to use then.

- If you want to travel during peak season (generally) March and November, you will need to earn 10,000 more miles by using your card.

The Citi Advantage Platinum Select MasterCard is also a good credit card to take while traveling, because the annual fee of $95 is waived for the first year, and there is no foreign transaction fee.

The other large American based airline is Delta. Generally, you need 60,000 Delta Sky Miles for a roundtrip ticket from the USA to Spain. Delta has an exclusive partnership with American Express. If Delta is the best airline for you to use based upon your home location, then we recommend that you consider an American Express card. Just be aware that you should also have a Visa or Mastercard for use in Europe to charge items and services, as the AMEX cards are not accepted everywhere.

The AMEX card for Delta that closely matches our favorite cards for United and American is the Gold Delta SkyMiles Credit Card.

Since its initial bonus is smaller than other cards, you will need to start using this card more months before you plan to travel to build up the needed SkyMiles. However, Delta does allow you to use miles plus cash to purchase a ticket. Some its features are:

- Earn 30,000 Bonus Miles after you use your new AMEX card to make $1,000 in purchases within your first 3 months.

- Also, earn a $50 credit in your account after you make a Delta purchase with your new Card within your first 3 months.

- Earn 2 miles for every dollar spent on eligible purchases made directly with Delta.

- Earn one mile for every eligible dollar you spend on purchases.

- Check your first bag free on Delta flights.

- Settle into your seat sooner with Main Cabin 1 Priority Boarding.

- Enjoy a $0 introductory annual fee for the first year, then $95 after that.

- No foreign transaction fees.

Cheapest Days to Fly

Flights are cheaper on Tuesdays or Wednesdays, so if you can be flexible about your fly dates, check out ticket prices on these two days of the week. We have found significant savings by flexing to fly on these less busy days for air travel.

Flights Open for Booking 330 Days Out

Once you have read all of our travel tips, decide on the date you want to travel. Following industry protocol, airlines first open up tickets for your travel date 330 days before the flight date, and this is your best chance at getting cheap ticket prices, or using frequent flyer miles to get a ticket. We don't know why this is so, but it is one of those airline mysteries we don't feel a need to understand. Use this tip whether you pay with cash or miles.

Good Airfare Prices Six Weeks Out

If you don't have as much lead time to plan your trip as mentioned above, then your next best chance at good prices is six weeks out from your travel date. Ticket prices begin dropping as airlines become eager to fill as many seats as possible for their flights.

Save Money by Traveling During the "Shoulder Seasons"

What are the shoulder seasons? The calendar dates before and after "peak" or "high" season will have significantly lower ticket prices in general. For your Camino trip, compare shoulder season ticket prices (April/May or September/October) with the peak of summer (June through August). We have always found the shoulder season prices to be hundreds of dollars lower. Off-season prices are even cheaper (November-March for the Camino). Walking the Camino during the off-season is not appealing to some people because of the winter weather and fewer open accommodations.

Budget Airlines

One way to fly near to St.Jean Pied-de-Port (SJPP), thereby saving travel time, is to fly into a major city that has budget airlines connecting to Biarritz, FR. Biarritz is only about an hour drive from SJPP, and you can choose a taxi, bus, or train service to get there. Bus and train service are the cheapest, but you must travel on their schedules. Always allow at least a day in between arrival at the major airport and your connection with a budget flight in case there is a delay in the long flight. We have flown direct from the

Eastern USA to London using miles to pay for the tickets, spent a couple of nights with friends in London, and then used some inexpensive tickets on Ryanair from London-Stansted to Biarritz. From there we shared a taxi to SJPP. Check the prices of flying into several major cities (Madrid, Barcelona, Paris, London) and then compare the differences in cost and travel time to get to your departure city to begin walking.

Tips for flying out of London-Stansted: The Stansted Express train leaves every 15 minutes from Liverpool Street Station, and cost 19 Pounds for a one way ticket. We recommend that you arrive at Stansted 3 hours ahead of your flight time. (This would be true for any flight departing Stansted, including Easy Jet, as they all share the same security checkpoint.) A shock for some first time budget air travelers is that as non-EU residents, Ryanair requires that you print out your boarding passes, rather than use their smart phone app boarding pass. This means printing them out before you get to the airport, or printing them out at a check-in kiosk at the airport at a cost of 15 pounds each! Bring security approved snacks with you as there are no complementary snacks on the flight. Our light packs fit easily in the overhead bins. The seats were comfortable enough, but did not recline, which we thought was okay for the short flight.

Want to Rent a Car or Drive?

If non-EU citizens plan to drive while in Spain, they will need a current in-force driver's license from their home country, and to rent a car you need an International Driver's license. Vehicular traffic drives on the right side of the road in Spain. This is especially important to keep in mind for walkers and drivers from countries where the traffic moves on the opposite side of the roads. Most fatalities of pedestrians/*peregrinos* are caused when someone from a country like England looks the wrong way before stepping out to cross the street, or when *peregrinos* forget to walk single file on the edge of roads facing oncoming traffic. Most car rental companies require an International Driver's License for non-EU drivers to rent a vehicle. We got ours at a AAA office in the USA.

You should also check your auto insurance policy to determine its coverage for international locations. This varies greatly. If you can afford to purchase the complete coverage offered by the rental company, we recommend that you take it as long as it allows you to hand in the keys on your return and not have any further hassle with a car that is damaged in some way.

Being There

E very Camino journey has the possibility of unexpected happenings and meetings, or what some call divine appointments. Prepare and plan as best you can, but make room in your itinerary and heart for these.

A Typical Day on the Camino

Walk, breathe deeply, hydrate, eat, rest, listen. Repeat. After walking on the Camino for a few days the rhythm of the journey centers on the pace of your stride, and the sound of your breathing. You are more aware of your surroundings than at home, because your surroundings are unfamiliar. The sounds. The smells. The temperature. The sun or rain. The light.

When you arrive at your destination for the night, whether it is an *albergue* or a hotel, check in, pay, and get your *sello* (stamp) in your *credenciál*. The reason for doing this at check-in is that it will allow you to get up in the morning and leave when you wish. *Albergues* almost always require payment when you register, but you might need to prompt a hotel desk to do this. *Albergues* usually allow check-in after 2 PM. During peak seasons you may see backpacks being queued up as early as noon as a way of holding a place until check-in. If you know the town you might stop tomorrow night, ask today's hospitalero for a recommendation of a place to stay, and then ask if he will phone ahead and reserve you a spot if that seems right to you. Find your bed, or go to your room and put down your heavy pack. Check the seams of the mattress for signs of bed bugs. If you see any, go get a refund and find another place to sleep.

Begin your wash ritual, which might be something like this. Take off your trail shoes and socks, slip on your Crocs, grab your fresh clothes (minus fresh socks), towel, valuables bag, and toiletries bag and head for the showers. We like some version of showering with your clothes on as a way to wash your clothes and body at the same time, conserving water. Peel off the wet clothes and rinse them and yourself well. Dry off. Put on your fresh clothes, and return to your bed. Wring as much water as you can from your wet things, and hang them up on the albergue drying racks or clotheslines, or use your safety pins to hang them up around your part of your bed if it's raining.

Begin your foot ritual. Remove any soiled dressings. Do a 5-minute foot soak in cool water or water with ice, if you have a source. Pat your feet dry. Elevate your feet for 10 minutes while they dry more. Apply new blister dressings if necessary (details in this book). Slip your Crocs on and explore a bit. If it is chilly wear a fresh pair of socks with your Crocs, and then use these in the morning. Buy any snacks or water you might want and decide where you will have dinner. Meet up with friends for a beverage and snack before dinner. This is also a good time for a nap if you are so inclined, or at least lie down and elevate your feet for rest. Some gentle yoga type stretching is ALWAYS a good idea.

Some *albergues* and hotels have cafés and restaurants, but otherwise you will need to search nearby for a place serving dinner at a time appealing to the early-rising peregrinos. Many eating establishments advertise a *Menú del Día* (Menu of the Day), or *Menú de Peregrino* (Pilgrim Menu) which they begin serving around 7 PM before customary Spanish dinner times, which are usually not until 9:30 or 10 PM. The typical pilgrim menu is three courses including choice of salad or soup, meat, dessert, and includes your choice of water or wine. The cost ranges 8-12€. Some *albergues* offer a communal meal, but even when you choose a café or restaurant, your host will often seat you with other *peregrinos*. These can be some of the most fun social times you will have on your trip.

Begin your going-to-bed ritual by 9 PM, as lights out for a communal *albergue* is 10 or 11 PM. Many *peregrinos* will be asleep before lights out, and since you are sharing space and taking turns in the bathrooms it makes sense to allow some extra time. Make a pillow for yourself by stuffing some clean, soft clothes inside a tee shirt or other soft item. A headlamp comes in really handy for reading in bed, but should be turned out at lights out so as not to disturb neighbors. (If you have to get up after lights out and need your headlamp to see, hold it in a closed hand to block as much light as possible from shining in your neighbors' faces.) Sleep in some of the clothes you will wear the next day to walk in, and load your pack with everything you can before going to sleep. Keep your valuables bag safe by putting it inside at the foot of your sleeping bag or sleep sack. Put in your earplugs. The **Mack's Ultra Foam Earplugs** we recommend are VERY good, and super helpful for canceling out most of the snoring and rustling of other *peregrinos*.

Begin your morning routine of dressing in your bunk and visiting the bathroom for your morning wash. Not all *peregrinos* will be as mindful of others as you will be, and some will begin the morning wake up routines earlier than you like. Someone usually turns on the ceiling light when it looks like at least half the peregrinos are up. Finish packing everything. *Peregrinos* must be out of *albergues* in the morning by 8 AM. If coffee or tea is available, enjoy some with friends. Otherwise begin walking and stop for coffee and breakfast later.

In warm months, most *peregrinos* get up and start walking early to finish before the extreme heat of the afternoon. Remember to pace yourself, stop to drink and fill up your water bottles at fountains along the way, and take rest breaks with a snack as you have need. Check with your *hospitalero* or guidebook to find out whether there will be a place ahead on the path to buy lunch when it is that time, and if not, be sure to have some snacks or a picnic lunch in your pack that day.

To get the most out of your Camino journey make plenty of room for spontaneous decisions or what some might call divine interruptions. Welcome interruptions as friends. Change what you can that needs changing, but have the grace to accept what you cannot change.

Helpful Phone Numbers for Spain

Using the phone in Spain will be much easier for Americans with a T-Mobile service plan like we use, which includes a good rate for cellular calls. Any time you are connected to wifi, you can make audio and video calls via the free Skype app or other video conferencing apps like FaceTime, but when internet service is poor or non-existent, being able to make a local or international *cellular* phone call for only 10 cents per minute is a really good thing.

Here are some emergency numbers we hope you do not need in Spain.

All emergencies

Call 112 (no area code needed)

Municipal police

Call 092

National police

Call 091

Tourist police in Madrid

Call 91 548 85 37

Emergency helpline in English, answered 8-24:00h

Call 902 102 112

Your Country's Embassy

Most countries have several consular offices throughout Spain. However, emergency consular services to citizens are generally provided by the main embassy only:

- **United States** Madrid Tel: 91 587 2200; https://es.usembassy.gov/u-s-citizen-services/local-resources-of-u-s-citizens/emergency-assistance/

- **United Kingdom** Madrid Tel: 91 714 6300; https://www.gov.uk/government/world/organisations/british-embassy-madrid

- **Ireland** Madrid Tel: 91 436 4093; https://www.dfa.ie/irish-embassy/Spain/

- **Canada** Madrid Tel: 91 382 8400; www.spain.gc.ca

- **Australia** Madrid Tel: 91 353 6600; http://spain.embassy.gov.au/

- **South Africa** Madrid Tel: 91 677 53 51 46; http://www.dirco.gov.za/madrid/en/

- **New Zealand** Madrid Tel: 91 523 02 26; https://www.mfat.govt.nz/en/embassies/

Where to Stay

If you have an unlimited budget, you may choose from the full range of accommodations along the Camino, from donation-only *albergues* (*donativo*) at the cheapest, most basic end of the spectrum to five star hotels at the other end, and every kind of lodging in between. Or maybe you are on a tight budget and hoping for cheap lodging every night. It is important to note that not every town has all the options. The only way to guarantee a bed for the night, especially during peak times for pilgrims like the summer, is to book ahead with *albergues* and hotels that take reservations, and then stick to that schedule. By scheduling ahead you forfeit a degree of spontaneity and freedom, but certain amenities or a cheap price tag might be non-negotiable for you. If you want to book ahead at a private *albergue* or hotel, many are listed on popular websites/apps. We used Booking.com most often. If you hope to reserve a bed in one of the cheaper places, which are usually not on a hotel booking site, a good way to do that could be to ask the *hospitalero* (host/manager) where you are staying to recommend a place ahead on your journey and ask them to call to reserve you a bed. Often you can reserve a bed this way, but the nature of the Camino is such that if you have not arrived by 3-4:00 PM to claim that reservation, it will probably be given away to someone else who walks in, unless you call around 2:00 PM to confirm that you are coming, and tell them when you plan to arrive.

The cheapest lodging, and there are only a few of these on the Camino, will be at the *albergues* designated as *donativo*, where pilgrims give what money they can in exchange for a bed. The most expensive lodging on the Camino are the four and five star hotels including the Spanish chain called Parador. Here is a glossary of terms:

Municipal albergues, or hostels, are government operated and offer dormitory style rooms with as many bunk beds as will fit in the space. 4-6€.

Parish albergues (*parroquia*) are operated by the local Catholic Church or diocese. Some offer a pilgrim mass and most serve a meal. 4-6€ or *donativo.*

Monastery albergues (*Monasterio* or *convento*) are run by either monks or nuns and vary in their facilities. 5-8€, some *donativo*

A variety of <u>associations and local governments</u> operate albergues along the routes. They are usually run by volunteer staff, many of whom have experience on the Camino. 6-8€

Private albergues are operated by individuals or groups, and vary greatly in their facilities, amenities, and number of beds. Amenities range from a bunk in a dormitory style room sharing a communal bathroom to semi-private and private rooms with semi-private and en suite bathrooms. The prices range from 8-40€. Breakfast is often included or available.

Hotels are operated by individuals, chains, and the government, generally have private rooms with en suite bathrooms, and range 35-130€ and up for a double room. Breakfast is often included.

It is worth mentioning again that companies do exist that will provide travel services to set up all of your accommodations for your Camino journey based on an agreed upon itinerary, schedule, and budget.

Transporting Your Pack

Even if you adhere to all of the advice about lightening your pack, there may be reasons you need help carrying it. It is good to know about pack transport services. You can pay 5-6€ to have your pack taken to the next place you will stay the night, and this can usually be arranged through your *albergue hospitalero* or the hotel desk. This will allow you to carry only your valuables (cash, credit cards, passport, smart phone) and essentials for your day hike (water, snack, rain jacket, sunscreen, extra socks). Our favorite transport service is *Jacotrans,* but *El Correos,* the Spanish postal service, is also now transporting packs.

Catching a Ride

If you need to stick to a schedule, and you find that you can't do it by walking, consider taking a bus or taxi one or more days rather than push yourself too hard walking and injure yourself by trying to keep up with a suggested schedule in a guidebook. Listen to your body. Take care of yourself and rest or ride when you need a break or need to catch up. Bus service is economical and serves every town along the Camino per their schedule, but taxis are more convenient.

Business Hours & Siestas

Spain uses a 24-hour clock to express time so much of the world calls 1:00 PM or 4:30 PM is called 13:00 and 16:30 in Spain. You will get used to this, but it may be unfamiliar to you at first.

A really good reason to carry a few small, lightweight snacks with you at all times, is that in smaller villages, some markets and stores close for lunch between 13:00 and 16:30. Typically small shops open 9:30-10AM, close for lunch, then reopen from 16:30-20:30. On Saturdays many businesses close at 13:00 for the day. Most businesses are closed on Sundays. Read about **"Spanish Holidays."**

Taking Care of Yourself

If you take the right approach to preventing injury and pacing yourself you will do well. When YOU are your transportation every day, you must learn to care for yourself in new ways. You can't take shortcuts caring for yourself without eventually paying the price with injury or illness, so be kind to yourself and take care.

Meals

Breakfast: Most albergues require you to leave by 8 AM. If they don't offer some type of breakfast, begin walking and stop at a market to buy something to eat as you walk, or stop at a café for a short breakfast and coffee. It's actually a good idea to have bought something the afternoon before for a snack so you can set out with maybe a coffee in your belly, then stop after a couple hours of walking for a mid morning breakfast and break. A traditional and delicious to-go breakfast is a wedge of tortilla Española, containing some combination of eggs, milk, cheese, and potatoes. Delicious, and it has enough protein to keep you going.

Lunch: Buy and carry; if you think you will want to eat along the Camino picnic-style try a *bocadillo jamón* (a baguette type of sandwich featuring Spanish ham), an *empanada* (meat or fish pastry), fruit and veggies that can travel, cheese, cured sausage, bread, cookies, nuts, chocolate, or yogurt. Any of these things work as snacks as well. If you do stop to eat at a café, another famous Camino lunch or light dinner is *ensalada mixta*, which varies every place you have it, but is usually a plate of lettuce, tomatoes, cucumbers, cooked beets, carrots, olives, and a hard boiled egg, and for additional cost some tuna (*atún*). Another common dish on most menus is *caldo gallego*, which is a soup (*sopa*) with some greens, onions, and some meat or chicken in a meat broth.

Dinner: You may have heard about typical Spanish meal customs, including evening meals that don't begin until after 22:00, and the stories are true! But along the Camino things are different for pilgrims. Cafés, bars, and restaurants serving *peregrinos* usually offer pilgrim menus being served as early as 18:00-18:30. A *Peregrino* Menu consists of three courses plus a beverage: soup, salad, or pasta for your first course, meat or fish for the second, then dessert, and either water or wine (not both) for around 8-12€.

Cooking for yourself: *Peregrinos* do cook for themselves, and it can be very economical, but sometimes it isn't feasible due to location, and lack of markets and cooking equipment in your *albergue*. An easy, inexpensive, lightweight meal that can work in a pinch by just adding some boiling water is some type of noodle or pasta bowl, but if you can handle it financially, try the evening *peregrino* menu for value and convenience, and provision yourself with breakfasts and lunches using market take-away and portable snacks, and stops at cafés and bars along the way. Remember that you should not take your own food into a café, or even sit outside in a chair belonging to a café without buying something there. This is how they make their living, *so peregrinos* need to respect that. The same goes for using bathroom facilities. You should use the bathroom (*servicio, toilet*) only if you are a customer.

Water

When returning pilgrims get together a lively debate may ensue about the best way to carry water: water bladders, purchased plastic bottles for hikers with a variety of drinking spouts, or our recommendation—a disposable, recyclable plastic water/soda bottle.We have used them all. A popular 3-liter water bladder system can fit nicely in your pack, and works well enough, but having used one on a Camino trip once, we would not use one of these again. If you choose one of these remember it is not necessary to fill it full whenever you refill, but it's more weight than we want to carry even empty. Re-usable sports bottles can work fine, but are not necessary. To be safe, both of these systems require thorough, regular cleaning, and that is not easy on the Camino, especially with the bladders. We like buying a 20-ounce beverage in a disposable bottle with screw top, or two bottles for longer stretches where you might need more water before a refill is available. After using it and refilling it at fountains and *albergues* along the route for a couple of days, you just toss it in a recycling bin, and buy a new one. This also cuts down on what you bring from home, and what you have to take back. If you really want to use a purchased sports bottle of some sort to refill along the way, please figure out a way to clean it regularly as you walk.

How much water do you carry? Water is HEAVY! An old rhyme says: A pint's a pound, the world around. (Sixteen fluid ounces of water weighs ~16 ounces.) A gallon weighs ~8 pounds. So a quart of water (32 ounces) weighs two pounds. A 20-ounce bottle is sounding better all the time, isn't it? The bottle weighs almost nothing, and 20 ounces will provide enough water to drink for a couple of hours, which is the usual distance between potable water sources, whether that is a roadside pilgrim fountain, a café, or even a private home, if you're desperate. Remember your "please and thank-you's" and smile. How much water you need per day, or for your distance for the day will depend on time of year and the weather and your needs. Drink up at every water stop and refill your bottle before leaving. Check with your *hospitalero* and experienced pilgrims each night to ask if you need to carry more water than usual the next day because of a longer stretch between water sources. (BTW, if you begin to experience darker than normal urine, or have a lot of pain in your joints and tendons, or get headaches it can mean that you are not staying hydrated enough. Drink plenty of water.)

When Nature Calls on the Camino

Answering the call of nature on the Camino makes for good story telling later. Communal bathrooms in *albergues* are a new experience for most North Americans. Most have gender divisions, but some do not. If you ever find yourself in a situation in which you feel that your safety is threatened, call for help, or quickly find help from other *peregrinos*. You might be unfamiliar with this difference in modesty, or body consciousness, with most of the world being much more relaxed and at ease with themselves. Hopefully your communal bathrooms will have doors or curtains on shower and toilet stalls, but you should always take your own "toilet tissue." Some places will have it, but most will not. We recommend taking the small travel packs of Kleenex tissues, called *pañuelos* in Spain. Take a couple packs with you from home to begin your walk, and replenish your supply at any market along the Camino.

These are much easier to pack and use than toilet paper on a roll. This also follows the general principle we give *peregrinos* in the planning stage: Buy what you can in Spain rather than carry things like this with you.

While you are actually out on the trail with no civilization around, you will want to find a private spot off the path to answer your call. With the increased numbers of *peregrinos* walking, cleaning up after yourself is what every considerate *peregrino* needs to do. Use a disposable grocery bag from your last purchase on the trail, or take some dog waste bags from home to pick up and discard your waste rather than leave it. Some towns have had to post signs warning *peregrinos* not to leave their waste behind, because it has gotten to be such a problem.

As mentioned in other sections of this guide, if you want to use the toilet at a store or café, you must be a customer. Facilities are for their customers, so you should compensate them by buying something.

Keeping clean

Wear your clothes into the shower, soak yourself with water, turn off the showers to suds up every where; strip off your clothes, scrub any areas of your clothes and body needing special attention, turn the shower back on and rinse everything thoroughly. Take off your wet things and wring out as much water as possible. Dry off your body with your towel or pareo. Dress in your fresh clothes, collect everything, go hang your wet things to dry, and tend to your post shower grooming and foot care ritual. This method keeps you and your clothes clean and conserves the water supply which can be strained during the summers in Spain. Washing out your clothes in this way won't get them as clean as washing them in a washing machine, so every few days, when you have access to laundry machines, use them to get clothes really clean. Bigger cities may have some "wash-dry-fold" shops that will wash and dry a bag of dirty clothes for a reasonable price.

We prefer to keep our washing routines simple on the Camino by taking **Camp Suds** to wash everything—our bodies, hair, and clothes. Buy a 16oz economy size bottle, then fill up a couple of 3oz **GoToobs** to take with you.

Be Well

Much is written about preventing or treating the most common injuries on the Camino: sunburn, blisters, overuse strains of feet, ankles and knees. Our favorite resource for Camino first aid is a free download written by Tom and Em Hill of Arizona. These two Camino veterans are also trained Community Emergency Medical Responders (CEMR), and dispense helpful information on prevention and treatment in a thorough, entertaining way. They include excellent diagrams and descriptions of injuries to help you diagnose and treat yourself, and tell you when to seek professional medical help. An excellent resource! Store the PDF version of the book in your smart phone library for reference along the way, even when you do not have wifi. Go to ***http://www.CaminoProvisions. com/First_aid*** to download. An observation from the Hills is that many injuries on the Camino happen when *peregrinos* follow the set itineraries in Camino guidebooks! Their point is, and we agree, that many injuries happen when a *peregrino* sets out to keep the pace laid out in a guidebook rather than personalizing their pace so they don't hurt themselves.

Bring any prescribed medication with you to last for the duration of your trip, as it is sometimes impossible to fill prescriptions in Spain. *Farmacías* are located conveniently throughout cities, identified with a green cross on their sign, but are often not available in smaller villages. Be prepared to treat food-related discomfort by taking antacid tablets with you from home, since this over-the-counter remedy is not readily available in Spain. As a stop gap for someone who has minor stomach upset and doesn't have something to relieve it, ask for an after dinner "digestive" in any bar, and they will give you a small glass of an herbal liqueur that might alleviate your symptoms. In addition to traveling with antacid tablets, we recommend having a few doses of an anti-diarrhea medication with you.

A good thing to know about Spanish emergency medical care is that there is no penalty for calling an ambulance in Spain if you are feeling very ill or concerned about another pilgrim's well being. A few deaths do occur each year on the Camino. Sometimes these are heart related issues present before the person left home, and made worse by the exertion or heat of the walk.

Other injuries or deaths have been caused when pilgrims are hit by cars because they did not look properly before crossing streets, especially in cities. Most at risk are people coming from a country where they are used to traffic driving on the left side of the road. When the Camino route takes you onto a paved road, please do walk single file on the edge of the road facing oncoming traffic. In 2015 five pilgrims were killed in one tragedy when they were hit by a truck because they were walking side-by-side on the road rather than single file.

Be Safe

Personal safety might be on peoples' minds because of the tragic abduction and murder of an American pilgrim on the Camino several years ago. While this is a rare occurrence, it happened. In the wake of this death, Spanish law enforcement has increased their attention to certain sections of the Camino Francés. Many men and women walk alone as pilgrims, and when precautions are taken, all should be well. If you ever feel threatened or unsafe, walk back and join other pilgrims until you feel safe again. Phone the police if you are threatened. Take a picture of a threatening person and report him.

A fear of Spanish dogs and other wildlife is circulating in some forums. We have never had a problem from local dogs, and no one we have interviewed has either. Farm dogs bark at passing walkers. This is the job of a good farm dog, and as long as you keep walking and do not threaten them or encroach on their property, you should be fine. If a dog should get closer than is safe, use your walking poles to keep him at a distance, while you continue walking steadily out of his territory. Watch for snakes and scorpions in the underbrush when you go off the path to answer the call of nature. Another good use of your walking poles is to place them out ahead of you to walk through any tall grass or underbrush, and be sure to stomp and make noise. Wildlife generally prefers to flee rather than encounter humans.

Stay aware of your environment and who is around, and take precautions like you would when you travel anywhere. In some places, and particularly in bus and train stations, thieves do operate by targeting international travelers, particularly westerners, and they may try to scam you for help "because they lost their ticket," "or the ATM took their card," or they "want to take a survey," etc. Better not to give money to anyone like this, but if you are inclined to help, offer to buy them a snack and coffee, and be careful when you take money out to pay for anything.

Most experienced *peregrinos* and *hospitaleros* agree that the Camino is safer than a walk most anywhere else, even your hometown. For many who have to fly to reach the Camino, the most risky time for theft is after leaving the Camino, because you have been in the special environment with others on pilgrimage who look out for one another. There are many stories of pilgrims leaving Santiago, arriving in Madrid to journey home, only to be pick-pocketed on the metro, or another crowded place. My son had his wallet, passport, and phone taken in just this way on the Madrid metro by professional thieves working together.

Avoid taking expensive gear, expensive jewelry, or other valuables with you on your journey, and when you need to charge your phone or other equipment, keep it close and in sight. Take advantage of electrical outlets when you stop for a meal, because the outlets at big *albergues* are in much demand. When unplugging your phone remember to take your charging cable with you. If you happen to forget it, tell the host at the next *albergue* or hotel and they might have one in the lost and found box that will work.

The best rule of thumb while you are on the Camino is not to leave valuables unattended. Keep your phone, camera, cash, passport, and credit cards with you at all times, and if you are traveling alone take them to the shower with you in your waterproof bag. Leave your backpack zipped shut and even stowed under your bed, and ask someone nearby to keep an eye on it for you while you shower. You can return the favor for them when they shower.

Sleep with your valuables in the foot of your sleeping bag or sleep sack, or under what you use for a pillow.

Scan or photocopy your passport and other travel documents and have them accessible on your phone, or printed on paper and secured in your backpack inner pocket.

Re-entry Into Life Back Home

For all of us at Camino Provisions, walking the Camino de Santiago and our continuing relationship with *peregrinos* all over the world has changed our lives forever for the better. The culture of the Camino carries is filled with God's light and love. And you don't have to be a Christian to experience it. Maybe there are other places on earth with trails more challenging, or vistas more breathtaking, but there is only one Camino de Santiago, which has been walked by millions of souls over a thousand years on a path sown with prayers, tears, and reverence.

While meaning unfolds in the process, the lessons learned during our Camino journeys continue to develop and bubble up into our consciousness long after we travel home. These lessons are welcome, but sometimes we don't know quite what to do with them. One of the reasons we started Camino Provisions was to foster community among those who have returned. Our FaceBook page is a place to receive encouragement in the freedom we learned on the Camino and want to live out at home. In turn, these are the very things that excite and encourage those who are in the dreaming and planning stages to make their first trip. We hear from those wanting to go and those who have returned that this is exactly what they need and hoped to find: returning *peregrinos* sharing with each other in a circle of information and encouragement that reflects the Camino journey.

Resources

Favorite Camino Websites

Online resources for the aspiring, English-speaking pilgrim

www.CaminoProvisions.com—Distilled information and wisdom from seasoned pilgrims; links to online outfitters store and links to pilgrim resources

www.AmericanPilgrims.com—source for free Pilgrim *credenciáles*, donations appreciated, membership optional; "APOC" is the nickname for this group; "fostering the enduring tradition of the Camino"

www.santiago.ca —the Canadian counterpart to APOC; helping Canadian pilgrims; *credenciáles*

www.csj.org.uk —The Confraternity of St. James in England is a fraternity of former pilgrims "interested in the medieval pilgrim routes through Spain and France to the shrine of St. James at Santiago de Compostela, and in the associated rich heritage of art, architecture, history, music and faith"; a source for much historical and cultural info on Spain, as well as guidebooks and *credenciáles*

www.csjofsa.za.org —The Confraternity of St. James, South Africa; "main aim is to assist South African pilgrims who wish to make a pilgrimage"; *credenciáles*

www.catedraldesantiago.es/en —The *Catedral de Santiago* official website; everything you want to know about the *Catedral* offered in several languages

www.peregrinossantiago.es/eng/ — The Pilgrim's Office in Santiago where arriving peregrinos go to register the completion of their journey and receive their Compostela; The office is in a beautiful facility in medieval Santiago at Rúa Carretas, 33.

www.pilgrimhousesantiago.com —An excellent website full of reliable information about Santiago; formatted in an easy-to-read layout; **Pilgrim House** is located at Rua Nova 19, a few steps from the Catedral. The good people at Pilgrim House offer a complimentary gathering place for pilgrims with comfortable seating, laundry services, clean bathrooms, and a friendly atmosphere in which to meet your friends, print boarding passes, and fix a cup of tea. Seasoned *peregrinos* are on duty to help incoming pilgrims orient themselves and process their experiences in addition to giving the practical help already mentioned.

Camino First Aid—THE best downloadable Camino first Aid book EVER. Download it from our website onto your smart phone into your library so you can access it whether you have wifi or not. Not only do the Hills give great first aid advice specifically geared for the Camino traveler, they also give general Camino advice with an entertaining style and plenty of humor.

www.KaraandNate.com —Great tips for international travelers, and more detail about "travel hacking"; great advice from a young, but experienced couple.

Favorite Camino Forums and Groups

The information in active pilgrim forums can be overwhelming, but it can also be valuable if you are willing to dig for it. Data overload is one of our consistent responses to postings on these forums, but they can be helpful. Here are a couple of our favorites.

Camino Provisions/FaceBook: Tips and news posted regularly by yours truly; I jump in with advice and answers to questions, and manage comments and conversations to remove any rants or bullying that might be posted by others.

Camino Provisions on Instagram and Twitter: Follow us on social media for news and updates as they happen @CaminoProvisions

> **www.CaminodeSantiago.me**— The Camino de Santiago Forum; Santiago resident Ivar Rekve manages this site, that includes many pilgrim topics and even more opinions to look through

Favorite Apps

New Camino related apps come along occasionally, and we will review them on our Camino Provisions FaceBook page as we learn about them.

> **Rome2Rio.com**, Discover how to get anywhere by plane, train, bus, ferry, or automobile; download the app and use it to chart your itinerary, or changes in your plan while there; links to bus, train sites

> **Booking.com**, Online resource for researching and booking accommodations; download this app onto your smart phone and use it along the Camino as needed

> **AirBnB.com** Online resource for room, apartment and home rentals through local hosts; create an account

and download the app if you want to use this type of lodging service

Google Translate, Online free downloadable translation app that allows you to handwrite, type or speak a word or phrase to have it translated into Spanish (or more than 90 other languages), or vice versa. Also gives you the ability to point your phone camera at a sign and have it translated. Very handy for your Camino when you have access to the internet or can use cellular service. Google Translate app from iTunes or Google Play

Duolingo, Free downloadable language interactive instruction program

Provisions With a Purpose Program

Peregrinos arriving in the Cathedral square in Santiago, the Praza Obradoiro

Helping Pilgrims on the Camino de Santiago

We founded Camino Provisions to help more people make a personal journey on the Camino de Santiago. Sure we help you prepare and plan before you go, and encourage you to process when you return, but we also want to help *peregrinos* as they walk. To do that we came up with the idea of sending a portion of our profits to non-profit groups operating along the Camino. As our family and team members become more involved along the Camino, we have met with some of these groups volunteering their time and help to pilgrims. We know groups on the

Camino Francés, Norte, and Portugués, and we have given volunteer hours and financial support to some of them, but we are excited about the possibility of helping more groups by sending a portion of our profits to keep their doors open, make repairs and enhancements to their buildings, and provide funds to help in all the ways *peregrinos* need it as they walk and after they arrive in Santiago. With every purchase you make through Camino Provisions, you are helping to support these volunteer groups who help pilgrims.

How do we choose which groups to support? Our team stays in touch with the groups we already know to be trustworthy to find out what their needs are, and what kind of help they are hoping to receive. If they have a specific need, say $500 for plumbing repairs, or $100 to put toward their internet service bill, we will try to meet the need or a portion of it.

Any non-profit group working to help pilgrims along the Camino de Santiago may write to us at **info@CaminoProvisions.com** to tell us about themselves and what their needs are. Write to us and tell us how you help pilgrims so we can help you help them!

To be eligible to receive financial aid through *Provisions with Purpose* a group must:

- Have official non-profit status with the Spanish government or with the USA government.

- Provide services to *peregrinos* along one of the Camino routes in Spain.

- Send us a letter of introduction and a written request including proof of non-profit status.

- Account for the use of the funds given to them by *Provisions with Purpose* within the calendar year the funds were received, including photos and paid invoices where applicable.

CAMINO
PROVISIONS

Packing List at a Glance

- Country of origin passport, or EU citizen documents

- Credit card/ATM card

- Cash: home country and Euros

- Travel Medical Insurance documents or European Health Insurance Card

- Smart phone

- Phone charging cable

- Electric outlet adapter for Spain

- Small waterproof sack

- Downloaded and/or digitized Camino guides in phone library

- Downloaded travel apps

- Digitized travel documents on phone with password protection

- *Credenciál*/Pilgrim Passport

- Backpack

- 3 water repellent packing cubes

- Road-tested trail shoes

- "At ease" sandals/shower shoes

- 4 pairs socks

- 3 underwear briefs

- 2 bras (ladies)

- 4 shirts

- 2 pants

- Jacket, lightweight and waterproof
- Fleece jacket (seasonal)
- Hat for sun
- Hat for warmth (seasonal)
- Rain gaiters
- Bandana
- Sun buff
- Gloves (seasonal)
- Traveler Nordic Walking poles
- Sleep sack or sleeping bag
- 1 Pareo/sarong (ladies) or travel towel
- 4 Emergency ponchos
- Prescription medicines
- Ibuprofen tablets or other pain relief tabs
- 2 3oz. GoToobs filled with Face and Body Moisturizer that includes SPF
- 2 3oz. GoToobs filled with Camp Suds for washing your body, hair, clothes
- Travel toothbrush and 3oz. toothpaste
- Travel size deodorant
- Ladies, enough feminine products for first two days of your period
- Travel hairbrush or comb

- Sunscreen towelettes

- Blister prevention/treatment items

- 3 travel packs Kleenex/Panuelos

- 6 large safety pins

- needle and thread

- small roll duct tape

- 5-10 pairs Mack's earplugs

- Eyeglasses/contact lens gear

- Sunglasses

- Shaving stuff

- Trail Toes anti-chafing product

- Nail clippers

- 3X5" spiral bound notepad

- Ballpoint pen

Packing Strategies

- Use a pack that will fit in the overhead bin of your aircraft to avoid lost luggage and make for easy boarding and de-planing

- Remove all hidden weight: Packaging, labels, unnecessary pages from guide book cut out (not torn), unnecessary clips and straps from gear like backpacks

- Use mini versions of things like toothbrush and toothpaste, hairbrush or comb; take minimal amounts of personal care products and replenish from shops when you run out; ladies, have enough supplies for the first couple of days of your period in case there is no market near you when it begins, but then buy what you need in the next place selling these supplies; if you run out of CampSuds and cannot find it in Spain when you need it, buy a regular size shampoo, refill one of your GoToobs, and donate the rest to the albergue; do the same thing when you need laundry soap, and fill your other GoToob

- As you pack at home, and re-pack along the Camino, ask these questions about each item: what would happen if I don't take this? Can I remove anything to lessen the weight without affecting the function? Can I replace several items with one that works for all? If you do not take something, but decide you need it when you get there, you will probably be able to buy it in Spain.

- As you walk the Camino, completely empty your pack every 3 days to see if there is anything you can throw away or mail ahead to your destination Post Office; is there any souvenir you could mail home cheaply?

- Use the Eagle Creek packing Cubes to organize your clothing and personal items; when you pack your clothes, roll each item up separately. This decreases wrinkling, and makes for easier access as you choose one item at a time rather than having to take out a stack of folded items

- Be sure to have important documents in a waterproof sack with space for your phone

- Pack your earplugs, needle and thread, and safety pins in an empty medicine bottle or GoTubb to make them easy to locate in your pack.

- Pack liquids, gels in a TSA approved quart-sized bag to get through airport security

- Pack your walking poles: Collapse your poles down to their shortest length and pack inside a free USPS or similar Priority Mail Tube, seal and label with your name, then check as baggage. Make sure the Baggage ID is affixed well and you have your claim ticket stub.

Made in the USA
Middletown, DE
19 November 2019

79026526R00055